Praise for
Employable

'Rocket engineer or hat maker, this passionate in-depth book will help you hone your skills, unleash your best qualities, drive your pathway and turbocharge your career to its ultimate success. A must-read for every step in your professional life.'

Julia Ross, Managing Director, Julia Ross Group

'This is an essential book because it addresses a crucial trend that affects us all. What made us employable previously is not likely to be what makes us employable now or in the future.

'Written with clarity by someone who has been matching people to jobs for many years, this book unpacks the key attributes that make one employable, and then provides a complete road map on how to stay current and ready for the best opportunities.

'It's a lively and practical read, an essential weapon in the battle against job uncertainty or insecurity. Full of anecdotes and practical examples, this book uncovers the "secrets" to employability! Roxanne is a deep expert in this area with 25 years of experience. And it shows!'

Greg Savage, Recruitment expert

'*Employable* is an easy-to-read handbook that covers everybody, not just the usual target of school leavers or graduates. Anyone can benefit from this book, even if you're not looking for a job change right now. There are interesting stories, personal anecdotes and the all-important practical advice to consider when thinking or re-thinking a career choice. But I also enjoyed the book just for its sheer "readability".'

Dr Sue Slowikowski, Undergraduate Advisor and Public Relations Lecturer, School of Business, University of Wollongong

'Rox Calder has always had a special connection with her clients. She looks at the person and the process from a holistic perspective and takes time to understand the characteristics of each person. Rox finds a way to bring their strengths to the forefront and to strengthen areas of less security, resulting in a confident, well-rounded candidate employers yearn for. Thoughtful, kind, clever and insightful, Rox covers all the prerequisites and adds so much more to ensure you can stand out and put your very best foot forward. As an experienced professional recruiter, Rox shares her invaluable insight, knowledge and advice on how to ensure you are at the head of the queue when it comes to employability. From attitude to skill set, presentation to communication, this book will show you how to be memorable for all the right reasons.'

Dijanna Mulhearn, Author of the *Wardrobe 101* book series

Employable

7

ATTRIBUTES TO ASSURE YOUR WORKING FUTURE

ROXANNE CALDER

MACMILLAN

I dedicate this book to my family, always my family.
George Calder, Ann Calder, Natalie Calder,
beautiful Rick and BFF Daisy.

First published in 2023 by Major Street Publishing Pty Ltd

First published in India 2023 by Macmillan
an imprint of Pan Macmillan Publishing India Private Limited
707 Kailash Building
26 K. G. Marg, New Delhi 110001
www.panmacmillan.co.in

Pan Macmillan, The Smithson, 6 Briset Street, Farringdon, London EC1M 5NR
Associated companies throughout the world
www.panmacmillan.com

ISBN 978-93-95624-97-8

1 3 5 7 9 8 6 4 2

Internal design by Production Works
Printed in India by Gopsons Papers Pvt. Ltd., Noida

Contents

Foreword by Heather Swan **1**
Preface: My path to employability **3**
Introduction: What is employability? **9**

PART I – THE 7 ATTRIBUTES OF EMPLOYABILITY 21

1. A thirst for knowledge **25**
2. Dependability **39**
3. Resilience **53**
4. Interpersonal nous **65**
5. Self-awareness **81**
6. Self-confidence **95**
7. Optimism **109**

PART II – MILESTONES AND LIFE 119

8. Graduates and school leavers **123**
9. When life gets in the way **141**
10. Parents returning to work **151**
11. To retire, or not? **161**

PART III – THE EMPLOYABLE TOOLKIT 173

12. Custom-build your résumé and cover letter **177**
13. Ace the interview **195**
14. Where to from here? **211**

About Roxanne **217**
Acknowledgements **219**
References **221**
Index **228**

Foreword by Heather Swan

Most people would not consider climbing and jumping from a Himalayan mountain a good career choice. Yet it was for me. This, along with other adventures such as flying a wingsuit across the Grand Canyon, has enhanced my 'employability factor' enormously.

Who would have thought it?

Roxanne Calder would have.

If you want a long career, one you design not only to provide an income but also to enhance your whole self, your wellbeing, your sense of self-worth, your purpose and your happiness – read this book.

Roxanne will show you how to understand who you are, what you want, where you are now, where you want to be and how to bridge that very important – and sometimes very big – gap.

Why? Because she has devoted herself to helping countless people do just that. She's taken all those stories and experiences, all those lessons learned, and distilled them into a 'how-to' that works.

I've known Roxanne for more than a decade. I've seen her take on big challenges and confront big fears. I've taken her and her recruiting team head way outside their comfort zone – rock climbing, skydiving and even into the remote outback, where self-reliance is critical. I've watched Roxanne struggle with her fears and win. I've seen her apply that same grit in the business world while never losing her optimism and passion for what she does.

Roxanne understands the importance of standing firm in the face of obstacles and self-doubt. She knows that to have the career you want, you have to grow your comfort zone and yourself, not just the obvious business skill set. She has an uncanny talent for helping people find their way.

When my daughter went to Roxanne for help finding an office job, Roxanne found her a dog-walking position instead, a position she still has and loves years later. Roxanne has mentored countless people in the same way – helping them choose their true passion and make that choice a success.

Having a copy of Roxanne's book is akin to having her truthful, caring, reassuring voice on call. This alone is worth so much more than the cost of a book.

Heather Swan, world-record-holding BASE-jumper and wingsuit pilot, mountaineer, author and motivational speaker

Preface: My path to employability

It was my first year at Monash University. I was lucky to be living on campus at one of the best universities in Australia, being exposed to a multitude of different people, courses and experiences and studying for a Bachelor of Arts, which I knew would interest me. I recall the relief of getting into a decent university and thinking, 'Phew, now I'm okay, hard work done!' Little did I know that the journey of forever being employable had only just begun.

I remember a conversation during my first three months at university. Vicky was a third-year student on my floor who was doing a Bachelor of Arts like me. She asked me what degree I was doing and then proceeded to tell me, at great length, that my degree was useless and wouldn't land me a job when I graduated. She, herself, was uninspiring – a little negative and even a touch depressive to speak with. I couldn't distinguish at that moment between what I could learn from her, and what was her own baggage.

We never spoke again, but her lecture/unsolicited advice stayed with me for the length of my degree.

Vicky was right to a certain extent. While I was annoyed at what I saw as her audacity, I have been grateful ever since. What she did was plant a seed, which I fed unconsciously with incremental actions. I chose subjects that might leverage my future job possibilities. One of these subjects was Human Resources (HR), which

I took in my final year. Studying HR was new then – I loved the subject, and it was one I did well in.

LEARNING MORE THAN JUST A LANGUAGE

My other main subject was Japanese. Now, I was far too relaxed at university to have excelled at learning Japanese. Studying any language needs constant and consistent application and work – you can't cram it. Despite my apprehension, I decided to take part in an exchange program, which involved studying at a prestigious university in Japan – all in the name of keeping me on that path to 'future employability'.

I can tell you honestly, I didn't want to use my summer break by going to Japan. I was not a diligent student. I was 20 years old. After my first year at university, I had settled more into university life than into university studies. I would have preferred to be at the beach or the pub having summer fun with my friends, rather than staying at the homes of various Japanese families and going to university daily.

I went because, somehow, I knew it would be good for me – a little like choosing to eat a salad rather than a burger. The trip to Japan assisted me greatly with my language skills and opened my mind to a different culture and customs – and I knew it would look impressive on my résumé in the future.

By the time I graduated from university, at the height of the 1990s recession, jobs were scarce. I didn't want to mope around and do any old ho-hum job. Instead, I wanted to stay on a path of employability and continue upskilling. So, I took myself off to Japan with the purpose of fine-tuning my Japanese language skills. My plan was to stay for 12 months – but I ended up extending my trip to three-and-a-half years.

In the beginning, I was happy to have any job and started in hospitality, at a five-star hotel in a beachside town called Atami. My job was as a 'meeter and greeter', and I worked six days a week. It was the norm in Japan, and all of us 'meeters and greeters' did it. Our job was to bow all day, every day – when someone entered, when they left and re-entered and then finally when they left for good. Very important job. On one side of the entry were all the petite and serenely beautiful Japanese girls lined up in their soft blue-flowered kimonos, and on the other side were the gents in their grey and blue (flowerless) kimonos.

I was with the Japanese ladies, of course, until I didn't fit anymore – literally as well as culturally. I ate so much Japanese curry (most people associate the Japanese with sushi, but their curry is very popular!) that I could not fit into my ladies' kimono. Instead, I was hastened into the men's kimono but, quite frankly, it was a disaster. I was then 'promoted' to the job of dishwasher in the hotel café. At first I was miffed, until I discovered we were allowed to eat ice cream during the quiet times. A silver lining. This experience was my first introduction to the importance of 'fitting in' at an organisation, and how quickly things can go pear-shaped if you don't.

Following my dishwashing stint my vocations began to improve slightly. While my roles were all casual in style, they were helping me to achieve my goal of speaking fluent Japanese. Along the way, I also developed so many other skills and attributes that complemented my degree.

My time in Japan taught me an important lesson: while we may not know exactly how at the time, ultimately all our actions and efforts will lead somewhere. Inactivity and non-exploration is undoubtably a much easier path to choose, but it's not the way to secure our future.

Working and living in a foreign country, where English is not the main language, for that period of time was tough. My resilience and tenacity were tested and strengthened. The environment was unfamiliar on every cultural level – from views on women, marriage, Australians and foreigners, to beer, food, sleeping, religion – you name it, it was all poles apart from what I knew. I had to negotiate jobs, contracts, visas, bank accounts, living arrangements, car licences – all in Japanese. At the time, I didn't think of it as an ordeal.

It just had to be dealt with if I wanted to be there. The unknown is sometimes uncomfortable, but it's also exciting, and I relished the thrill of trying to make things work, no matter the obstacles.

Towards the end of my stay in Japan, I became acutely aware of the unexpected benefits of living within limitations. I was discovering something new about myself every time I encountered a new challenge. I came to understand our inborn, human ability to persevere and create solutions instinctively.

I returned to Australia fluent in Japanese, but with no motivation or desire to work for a Japanese firm in Australia. However, those three-and-a-half years in Japan made me the perfect candidate for a job in recruitment. The number-one strength you need to work in the recruitment industry is resilience (refer to chapter 3). After living in Japan, I had this in abundance! During my travels I found there were very few setbacks that I could not deal with. I had to deal with all the stresses and challenges and solve all my problems myself – there was no-one else to fix things for me.

When you live in a foreign country where you must speak in a second language, all your senses become heightened. I became acutely attuned to read body language, interpret eye contact and recognise subtle messaging. For the first time, I became fully aware of what observing and being an observer means, and how powerful it can be. I surprised myself by how much I embraced my newfound observer role, considering I am not naturally patient.

I had to learn the art of observation to survive. Although I might not have understood half of what was being said, I learned to pick up the subtleties of interaction and how to use these to negotiate and influence. These are skills that have served me to this day.

MY FIRST STEPS IN RECRUITMENT

Upon my return to Australia, I began what was to be a long and successful career in recruitment. My first job was with Julia Ross

– a well-known, inspirational entrepreneur, business magnate and founder of Julia Ross Recruitment. From the moment I interviewed with Julia, I wanted that job. I was enthralled by what she had achieved. I loved that she was a woman in business doing great things. There was a magical power and thrill about working there. I wanted to be a part of it!

Recruitment was tough, and working in a Julia Ross world was even tougher – standards were high. For the first time since completing my degree, I felt I was on track to having a professional career. My training was excellent – some of the best recruiters and managers at the time trained with Julia Ross. I know if it had not been for my experience with Julia, I would not be where I am today. I loved that job. It gave me a sense of belonging. I could have chosen a different recruitment company to work for, but I am not sure I would have been as enthralled and motivated in another firm. The values of loyalty, trust and having a strong work ethic, as well as Julia's high service levels and standards, innovative approach and willingness to strive for perfection, suited my personality and style.

The funny thing is, I fell into that job! I went for an interview at the Julia Ross Recruitment office in Parramatta for a job in banking and they suggested I might be suited to recruitment. They gave me a test: they said, 'We are advertising this weekend. Have a look out for the job ad.' (In those days, jobs were advertised in Saturday's newspaper.) I looked but couldn't see it. So, I called up on Monday and said I couldn't see the advert, but I asked to apply anyway. The rest is history!

JOINING THE DOTS

I wonder if Vicky, the third-year Arts student, would be surprised to learn that my 25-plus-year career in recruitment has taken me throughout Australia and to the UK, Singapore and Hong Kong. Perhaps she'd be even more startled to hear that this experience led me to complete an MBA and launch my own boutique recruitment firm, EST10, in 2010. So much for my 'useless' degree, Vicky!

As a young undergraduate, the concepts of lifelong learning and being employable were not something I gave any thought to, but my path to being employable had always shown in my actions and behaviours. I seemed to instinctually understand what I needed to do to make myself employable. It was only later in life that I started to pay close attention to the choices we humans make in life, and how they influence our future path.

Recruiters develop the ability to look at candidates and their résumés in terms of a 'life map story' – a map of the candidate's direction, with many connecting dots representing the whole picture. This provides invaluable insight into candidates' personalities, but also highlights their untapped potential.

I have always loved hearing stories of people who go against the tide and challenge our perception of what success is. I once read that Steve Jobs took a summer class in calligraphy, not knowing if it would ever have any value or application in his career. At the time, he had just dropped out of university and wanted to keep himself busy. In his own words, 'If I had never dropped out, I would have never dropped in on this calligraphy class, and personal computers might not have the wonderful typography that they do.'

Steve Jobs also said: 'You cannot connect the dots looking forward; you can only connect them looking backward.' In other words, you need to trust that the dots of your life and experiences will connect in the future. You don't always know which of your actions will change the course of your life.

If you cannot see how your dots connect yet, be patient. Sometime and somewhere, your personal and professional stories will come together in a beautiful arrangement, just like mine did.

Introduction: What is employability?

Employability is insurance for your future. It is future-proofing yourself, giving yourself the freedom to choose your own path. The concept of employability is crucial to understand and embrace if you are to stay current and relevant in this ever-changing time.

In its simplest terms, employability is what makes someone more likely to gain employment, keep employment and be successful in their chosen occupation. It's made up of a set of continual achievements: skills, experience, understanding and personal attributes. However, employability is complex – it's not just a 'tick the box' exercise. It is your mindset. It includes 'soft skills' and an understanding of how to put your transferable skills into practice.

Employability benefits everyone – the individual, the workforce, the community and the economy.

In my 25-plus years at the coalface of employment, I've found there is an increasing shortage of employable people.

Being employable is not the same as being employed.
Having a job does not necessarily mean you are employable.

No-one has an accurate idea or data to predict with certainty how the employment world will look in the near or distant future. That means that if you are privileged to be employed right now, looking at ways to reskill and upskill while within the safety of your job will go a long way to future-proofing your continued employment. The fragility of what the world experienced with COVID-19 has taught us that we must never sit on our hands. The responsibility lies only with you to make your professional development a priority.

If you are struggling to find work, you may benefit from reading this book in full, then taking stock of the areas you need to focus on. If you are a recent graduate, you need to be thinking about potential workplaces and evaluating your skill set for areas to develop. You have youth and time on your side – two benefits that are wonderful but pass quickly, missed by all who once had them!

In our current times, no matter whether you stay with your employer or change jobs and companies, knowing the attributes that make you employable will be imperative to your success.

It is dangerous to think just because you have a job you are employable. It's even more precarious to think just because you have a job you will forever have a job or work in that same company. Nothing lasts forever, which is the first lesson you learn in kindergarten. Yet, you might find that you still take things for granted or try to cling to conditions that long ago lost their usefulness or positive influence on your life.

UNCERTAINTY IS HERE TO STAY

We have recently witnessed a swift upskilling in using technology for remote working. Five years ago, would you ever have imagined holding meetings via Zoom, or having telephone or video appointments with your doctor? Occasionally, maybe – particularly if you are travelling overseas – but not as the new normal.

There are jobs now that we'd never heard of a decade ago. According to the World Economic Forum, 65 per cent of primary school children will end up working in new job types that aren't even on your radar yet.

Seven jobs that no longer exist

1. Human alarm clock
2. Lamplighter
3. Milkman
4. Night-cart man
5. Punch-card operator
6. Rat catcher
7. Switchboard operator

Seven jobs that are unlikely to exist in ten years

1. Cashier
2. Data entry operator
3. Legal secretary
4. Receptionist
5. Social media manager
6. Telemarketer
7. Travel agent

Seven jobs that didn't exist ten years ago

1. Blogger or vlogger
2. Cloud specialist
3. Drone pilot
4. Influencer
5. Listening officer
6. Social media analyst
7. Sustainability manager

Being employable is also about being 'on course' – aiming to be on par with or, ideally, a step ahead of your peers.

Without a skerrick of doubt, companies will be looking at totally different skill sets in the future. This will mean you need to act today and be ready for the change ahead of time. These actions don't have to be big – incremental shifts are all that is required. Mentally accepting this concept is your first step.

The only real certainty is that uncertainty is the new normal. As I write this book, we are coming out from under the shroud of COVID-19 and many economists, the press and politicians are saying this might be one of the toughest economic climates Australia has faced. Our world has changed in ways we could never have foreseen. We have not seen an employment market like this before. We're navigating an entirely different working arena, one where technology is key to survive and thrive and for the first time ever, we have five generations all working together.

Through my work in recruitment, I saw firsthand the devastation COVID-19 has wrought. Between March and June 2020, my company fielded daily calls from the unemployed – people desperate and helpless after losing their jobs and fearful of losing their livelihoods.

Being confronted with this brought home the reality of how fragile our world is and how much we rely and depend upon our jobs – whether we realise, acknowledge or like it. This is why I have written this book – to help you find new ways, new skills and new attitudes to ensure your employability, no matter what situation you find yourself in.

The COVID-19 pandemic is not the only framework for you to test your employability. Any instability, be it economic, social or simply disruptive, will spark the talent competition and benefit those who decided to invest in their own development, learning and growth. The moment in time when this is done is crucial. Early adapters always win.

The world rate of change has been accelerating rapidly for decades now, and if you feel anxious about that, you are not alone. According to research by global leadership company Accenture, 64 per cent of the global workforce is experiencing high anxiety over their personal job security.

Technology advancements will occur – there is nothing more certain. Even if you are young now and technology is second nature to you, don't assume you will always be across what is new. Make sure you do not feel too comfortable; challenge your agility and make sure you're regularly across new developments.

You always need to be employable – no matter where you are at, and no matter where the economy is at.

BE DELIBERATE ABOUT YOUR DEVELOPMENT

This concept of being employable is vital for anyone who relies on an income to support themselves. The days of lifelong tenure are long gone. In fact, depending on how old you are, you may never have heard of or witnessed this concept.

As I shared in the preface, I operated at an instinctual level for most of my early working life. However, thanks to the fact that my career depended on being acutely aware of all the necessities and changes in the employment landscape, I, too, started to see how essential it is to be employable. An occupational hazard/benefit, you could say!

The key is to shift from being instinctive to deliberate in your ongoing professional development.

You need to take full responsibility for your future career direction. Owning the process and consequences gives you a better sense of freedom, no matter the environment you find yourself in. It is the choice and not the 'accident' that will decide how successful you are.

In this zone, you are honing and fine-tuning the 'craft' of being employable. You don't have to be a hyper-dedicated, studious, nerdy, highbrow, ambitious, serious sort of person to be employable. You really can just be an improved you! Being employable belongs to you as much as anyone else.

BEING EMPLOYABLE DOESN'T JUST HAPPEN

Although being employable does not have to be difficult, it doesn't just happen. Effort, patience and practice are required.

You need to work at it. You have to do things you would rather not and make sacrifices and compromises. Employability means being in the uncomfortable zone sometimes. To learn, develop and improve takes effort, just like developing and strengthening a new muscle: it can hurt at the beginning, but then it grows and develops and becomes stronger. It may even cause enough pain that you start to rethink whether you should continue. Don't be fooled! This is the unknown, instinctive and irrational side of the brain, according to Jungian psychology.

It will take effort, time, consistency and endurance, but if you stop and then go back to it, which is also okay, you will have already developed what is popularly referred to as muscle memory. Like any well-formed and repeated habit, it does get easier, because the previous tough times tested your mettle and showed you that you could do it.

Like all journeys, sometimes it will be easy-peasy, freewheeling, even lackadaisical, and other times it may feel like a constant uphill battle. The uphill battles, though, are often the biggest opportunities. The learning they present to you can catapult you forward, much further than you'd travel stuck in cruise control.

Working on being employable will give you a sense of security, safety and freedom to choose. It is no different to looking after your physical health by choosing to eat well and exercise. By being employable, you are looking after your employment health.

REDUNDANCY: IT'S NOT ABOUT YOU (OR IS IT?)

During my career I've met with many good people who have been made redundant or sacked. They tell me their stories and, in some cases, I read between the lines and can see what has really occurred: their lack of joy and enthusiasm for their job is the reason we find ourselves discussing their next career move. Often they admit that they didn't particularly like their job.

Now, redundancy occurs when a role is no longer required. It's not to be used as a way to performance-manage a person out of an organisation. The reality is, though, when companies and hiring managers are choosing which roles are to be on the redundancy list, employability can count. As an example, if 20 customer service roles need to be cut out of a team of 50, your attitude and enthusiasm for your role could potentially be part of that decision.

To be clear, though, in a lot of cases redundancy isn't due to your employability – it's just what happens sometimes in life. In these cases, your employability will get you through the process of looking for a new role far more easily.

As previously mentioned, when I graduated, we were right in the throes of the 1990s recession. I had been fortunate enough to have a wonderful part-time job throughout my time at university – I worked at David Jones department store on Friday nights and Saturdays, and as many hours as I could during the university breaks. I didn't feel the recession while studying – my costs and expenses were low: alcohol, rent, food and petrol (in that order). We didn't spend much on clothes in those days – your wardrobe contained the stuff your parents would buy for you and you made it last.

When I graduated, I found a job in Daimaru, a new Japanese department store that had just famously opened in Melbourne. My experience at David Jones, combined with my degree and language skills, made it relatively easy to secure that job.

After around six months, Daimaru made more than 100 people redundant and I was one of them. I was devastated. I recall thinking, 'Why me?' I thought my university degree made me so superior to my peers, some of whom didn't even have a 'proper' degree. I am embarrassed now by my ignorance back then.

I can see now that I wasn't actually very employable while I was working at Daimaru. I had been employable enough to secure the job on graduating, when graduate jobs were so scarce, but I was young, inexperienced and not grateful enough to appreciate the job. The package of 'me' – my skills and attitude – wasn't competitive enough to keep my job in tough economic times.

I did not enjoy my job at Daimaru, and I am sure that contributed to being selected for redundancy. I had loved my old job at David Jones and was good at it. Would I have been made redundant if I had stayed there? I don't think so. I believe it is critical to love enough of your job to retain the enthusiasm, joy and motivation to be on the path of being employable.

WHAT ABOUT LONG-TERM JOBS?

I have interviewed numerous people who have left their jobs after, let's say, 10-plus years.

Personally, I love to see people stay with companies for a long time. It shows loyalty, relationship skills and consistency, plus it can also be great for learning and development.

However, a long-term tenure can also easily slip into a situation that isn't so great for learning and development. Some of the people I have interviewed fall into this category, and they find it exceptionally hard to secure their next role. This is a good example of being employed but not employable.

The difficulty lies in their grasp on the reality of the situation – that their skills may have slipped and they may not be as employable as they first thought. It is not a comfortable realisation and is often followed by feelings of rejection which, let's face it, can be very hard on all of us. It can be demoralising and the perfect situation for anxiety and, even worse, depression to occur. Our self-worth and even our whole identity is tied so closely to our jobs.

If people are quick in accepting the situation, the result can be much brighter. It's when the ego won't let reality come into view that there are consequences. The worst part of this scenario is the effect on self-esteem and confidence.

Imagine pulling a pair of old jeans from your wardrobe that you haven't tried on for 10 years. They fitted perfectly back then and you felt confident wearing them, but they are not quite the same now – a little tight around the waist, firmer than you recall around the thigh, not as on trend, maybe even out of date?

Maybe you haven't kept up your fitness, or maybe that style, which was so on point back then, is now yesterday's hero. Either way, you have some work to do!

I HAVE A DEGREE – ISN'T THAT ENOUGH?

As a final point in this introductory chapter, I want to touch on education, qualifications, degrees and the like. In my opinion they are important – I always like to hire people with a degree for my business – but I never rule out people if they don't have one.

For my employees it's a nice-to-have. A degree shows to me an ability to learn, to apply yourself, to think and work at something over a period of time – developing the resilience muscle, which is so needed in recruitment!

There are of course many ways to gain further education. In fact, if you're in Australia, you live in one of the luckiest countries in the world for education, where mature-age entry is easily accessible.

Qualifications are critical and necessary for certain jobs. However, buyer beware: they are only part of the equation.

Being employable is a continual journey of lifelong learning.

Your education and learning should be ongoing. This goes hand-in-hand with being curious, asking questions and looking to understand.

Attitude and personality also come into play. I have worked with too many people who have indeed had degrees and been exceptionally well qualified and smart, but they have not been employable.

Do not rest on your laurels if you have a degree. Use it and keep leveraging, learning and developing.

ABOUT THIS BOOK

This book will help you understand why being employable with conscious intent is important for your future – financially, spiritually and psychologically. It will help you acquire the tools to make employability a vital part of your working life's practice.

I have written this book for everyone – whether you are a school leaver, a university graduate, in your first job, returning from parental leave, a senior executive thriving in your career, a business owner, a managing director or someone like me – in your 50s, with a successful career in place, yet knowing there is so much more to do.

This book is for you, whether you're career-focused or someone who is happy to simply 'have a job': that is, go to work and come home. You may be comfortable in your job and have no intention of leaving, but that is no reason to take your finger off the employability pulse. Put simply, you never know what will happen. Life is unpredictable, but to frame it in a positive way, change enables growth and development. You can be comfortable and happy by staying in your comfort zone, if you choose, but life will always find a way to introduce you to unexpected events.

In this book, I'll take you through the process of evaluating your own employability, helping you devise an action plan to fill in the gaps.

In part I, we'll look at the 7 attributes of employability. These are the attributes that I have observed in my career as those that the most employable candidates possess, and you can use them to boost your own employability. I provide insights and expert advice from my career, as well as sharing those from a host of experts in business, HR, recruitment and leadership. I feel privileged to share the knowledge these experts have gained over many years and many lessons – their failures as well as successes.

In part II, we'll explore all the ways that life can get in the way of our best-laid plans! Family, births, marriages, health issues, concerns for children, ageing parents, financial matters and the like can all derail our career pathways. We'll also look at employability throughout the different stages of life. While the need to remain employable doesn't change, a school leaver or graduate is in a vastly different situation from a parent who is returning to work, someone in midcareer, a breadwinner who has just been retrenched or someone trying to decide whether to retire or not. We will unwrap some tools to fast-track the process of becoming employable at each of these stages.

The secret of change is to focus all your energy,
not on fighting the old, but on building the new.

–

DAN MILLMAN

In part III, we'll unpack the nitty gritty of employability – the tools you need to win that job. We'll look at CVs and target résumés, interview skills and cover letters. It's no longer enough to simply rinse and repeat the same old CV year in, year out.

From the files

Part of being employable is learning from your own, and others', mistakes. When it comes to jobs and careers, I have seen it all – in my role as a recruiter, and in my personal life. In this book, I share some practical examples of my

experiences and observations 'from the files' – stories that you can learn from and perhaps apply to your own life.
I hope you'll enjoy taking a peek into a recruiter's files.

Employability is a forever journey. For that reason, all the behaviours and actions that go into the journey of being employable will enrich your life in many other ways – your self-esteem, your confidence and your coping mechanisms, for starters.

Employability is ingrained in me, and I hope the information in this book will empower you to take control of what you want for your future.

TOP FIVE TAKEAWAYS

1. Uncertainty is here to stay – no-one is protected from disruptions to the economy, in their field or in global, national or local circumstances.
2. Employability is for everyone, whatever your stage in life.
3. Education and learning should be ongoing.
4. Employability gives you freedom by giving you control over your employment prospects. It is your insurance against the risk of unemployment.
5. Employability is an ongoing journey – qualifications help, but they are only part of it.

PART I

The 7 attributes of employability

Without work, life goes rotten,
but when work is soulless,
life stifles and dies.

–

ALBERT CAMUS

I HAVE OFTEN THOUGHT I may be in a small percentile of people who are lucky enough to work in a profession they love. I am fortunate enough to adore my job, vocation and career choice. Sometimes, I actually give myself a little pinch just to ensure I am not dreaming. However, I am not delusional – I know that you can't always love your job. There are times when the challenges almost seem too much, but luckily for me, so far love wins out.

When I first started working in recruitment, I couldn't believe I had landed a job I enjoyed so much and that I seemed to be quite good at. In those days, we were paid bonuses, and if you did well the bonuses were very good. I always did well. Every time I received a bonus I would ask myself, 'Would you still do this job if you didn't get paid the bonus?' The answer was always yes.

I often wondered about what would happen if there came a time when my enthusiasm and motivation for my job waned. Perhaps I was spoiled or ruined, but I was hooked on the joy of loving my job and I knew a life without that level of satisfaction was not for me.

What I have learned through my own employment experiences, and from speaking with so many people about theirs, is that your job heavily influences the rest of your world. If you take your career for granted, you might not be entirely aware of how crucial your job is to ensuring the rest of your life ticks over. Even at a basic level, your job generates an income that allows for the necessities and wants you have in your life: having a home, education, family life, experiences and health. It goes much further than that, though. I believe that being challenged in your job, feeling satisfied and content and finding meaning in what you do is critical for a life well lived. This is why it is so important to possess the 7 attributes of employability.

***

The 7 attributes of employability I've written about in this book are those I have identified during my 25-plus years in global recruitment as being essential for employability. When recruiting for clients, as well as for my own business, these attributes have been proven time and time again to be those that are necessary to be employed and remain employable.

Please do not expect to be able to immediately check off all these attributes as part of your natural personality. I have never encountered a person fortunate enough to be in this position. However, the very best of employees have these 7 attributes as a work in progress. Some will be part of your natural way of being, while others may require significant work. For me, resilience comes quite naturally whereas self-awareness is an attribute I have really had to work on. Because of this work, however, I'd say my self-awareness now surpasses all my other attributes in strength.

Being part of people's careers and witnessing their professional growth has been the biggest privilege of my working life. The one thing the most memorable candidates have in common is that they're all working on these 7 attributes. With the willingness to acknowledge their weaker attributes and with the right mentorship, these people have flourished in their careers and personal lives as well. After all, your job and personal life are interconnected.

All these attributes, no matter your experience or job, can be developed and nurtured, even those that seem insurmountable. You will be surprised by the joy and sense of achievement this process can bring.

1

A thirst for knowledge

We keep moving forward, opening new doors,
and trying new things, because we are curious,
and curiosity keeps leading us down new paths.

–

WALT DISNEY

Learning is the first and most important of the 7 attributes of employability. Being employable requires you to be continually learning and updating your skill set.

I refer to the thirst for knowledge attribute as 'forever learning'. Forever learning is:

- being curious
- listening
- being open to new ideas
- being willing to adopt and adapt to new ways
- finding ways to improve yourself and increase your experience and knowledge.

In this chapter we'll examine all the facets of this high-level life skill, including:

- personal and professional growth
- your ability and willingness to learn
- being curious
- keeping your technical skills current
- planning and upskilling.

PERSONAL AND PROFESSIONAL GROWTH

Having a thirst for knowledge is important – not just to your job and vocation, but as a life skill. Most people think of professional growth when it comes to employability, yet working on your personal growth can be the key to excelling. Personal development gives you the power to be who you dream to become, both personally and professionally.

> **You cannot grow professionally without personal growth and development. The further developed you are personally, the more rapidly you can excel professionally.**

Table 1.1 lists some ways in which you can grow, professionally and personally.

Table 1.1: Personal and professional growth

Professional growth	Personal growth
Setting goals	Learning about yourself; understanding your personal identity
Educating yourself	Developing self-awareness

Professional growth	Personal growth
Advancing skills specific to your job or career	Learning to understand the impact of your actions
Enhancing your existing skills	Learning about perception versus intention
Building professional networks	Developing emotional intelligence (EQ)
Planning your career	Discovering your trigger points (Kryptonite, as I refer to it!)

You may think it's easier to achieve personal growth than professional growth. I thought that once too. But fasten your seatbelt! Personal growth goes deep to who you are and can be like a rabbit hole, with more and more to discover. If you work on your personal growth areas with due respect and diligence, the process can be significantly harder than the professional-growth journey. Whether personal or professional, growth requires effort, practice and work. The payoff is that it is rewarding and enlightening.

THE ABILITY TO LEARN

Let's address the elephant in the room: many adults are concerned about their ability to learn. Did you know that believing you can become smarter actually makes you smarter? According to research from the American Psychological Association, realising that your intelligence may be improved can actually improve your intelligence. Also, understanding intelligence as something that is changeable and malleable, rather than stable and fixed, results in greater academic achievement.

We are all able to learn. Numerous studies have shown that learning is possible at any age – what may change, however, is the learning style. For example, a 1999 study of older adults found that not all older learners are 'active, hands-on' learners. With age comes a tendency to become more reflective and observational in the learning environment. More of the 55 to 65 age group preferred learning by feeling and doing, more of the 66 to 74 age group preferred learning by feeling and watching, whereas the 75 and older group preferred learning by thinking and watching.

In my experience, those who learn the best:

- are curious
- are willing to learn
- are disciplined
- accept feedback
- put the effort in.

The capacity to learn is a gift; the ability to learn is a skill; the willingness to learn is a choice.

–

BRIAN HERBERT

WILLINGNESS TO LEARN

If you are willing to learn, you can also achieve. Learning can happen reactively or proactively.

Reactive learning occurs immediately because of some sort of discomfort, such as pain or danger. I learned about reactive learning when I tripped over my shoelace in a netball game at school and broke my arm. Ever since, I have never had an undone shoelace. My shoelaces are double-knotted, and I can't help letting people know when I see their shoelaces are undone – even random strangers.

Proactive learning is a deliberate action. In his 2008 bestseller *Outliers: The Story of Success*, Malcolm Gladwell, claims that it takes 10,000 hours to achieve world-class expertise in a task or skill. While others have disputed this claim, mastering a task or skill often requires deliberate practice.

Everyone can learn, but for all of us – even the smartest – it takes willingness.

I believe that if you do not learn, it's because you have chosen not to, or because you have been heavily conditioned to have no belief in yourself or your abilities. If this is you, there are plenty of stories about highly successful people – actors, entrepreneurs and business-people – who were told they were not good enough or couldn't learn easily. Look them up – let's see how curious you are!

You don't have to regard yourself as 'naturally smart' or 'sharp' in order to learn. If you are using this as an excuse, you are self-sabotaging. Learning is how you *become* smart! Yes, some people are gifted and others possess a great capacity to learn, but the ability to learn is a skill that can be practised – effort plus time plus repetition.

From the files

Let's say the hiring manager has two candidates to choose from. One has a good understanding of a process or task but isn't adaptable or willing to keep learning and developing. The other candidate is 'average' at the same task but willing to learn.

Almost always, the hiring manager will choose the candidate with the willingness to learn. This may not have been the case 10 years ago but is undoubtedly true in today's employment market.

Change is constant. You need to be adaptable, agile and stay open to new experiences, and prospective employers expect this. The days of following processes to the letter are gone. Employable people look for ways to improve a process and solve problems that come their way. No-one has necessarily shown them how to do this, but through their ability to adapt, enquire and acquire knowledge, and do so quickly, they have learned how to navigate difficult situations.

If you can demonstrate your adaptability, ability and willingness to learn, your employer will be confident that you can handle the challenges that are constant in our world today.

CURIOSITY

'Curiouser and curiouser', a phrase from *Alice in Wonderland*, embodies my thinking about learning. The more you inquire, the more there is to know. The more you understand, the less you realise you know. So, you keep digging and delving! The opposite of doing this is remaining in ignorance. 'Ignorance is bliss' is wide off the mark if you want to be employable!

Think of the human body as a receptor. You are feeling, seeing, hearing and sensing all around you – every day, every minute – and you choose what to take in, what to question and what to ignore.

Technology can make it easy to access information, but it can dumb you down, too. If you are not careful, you can find yourself with a surface-level knowledge about a range of things but an in-depth knowledge of nothing. You need to become curiouser and curiouser!

When you are curious, you will investigate further. You are engaged and interested, and you keep going because you are motivated to do so. You put in the effort required to find out more, and from sources other than Wikipedia!

Being curious is critical, whether it's about a hobby or a work-related issue. The good news is that, metaphorically, curiosity is a muscle that you can stretch and grow. The more you inquire, the greater your understanding, and the closer you come to being an expert. The endorphins kick in and you become more excited, engaged, intrigued and motivated. You retain information without even trying! Because you're interested, you understand suddenly why X and Y occurred... because it was linked to Z. Have you ever been to a trivia night and wondered how some people know stuff that seems so obscure? It's because they are curious.

Curiosity keeps your brain functioning. Think of it as the necessary daily exercise for your cognitive health. The more you exercise it, the better it becomes. Your confidence levels will increase as will your self-esteem, both important attributes to being employable. The reason people do puzzles or crosswords, especially in retirement, is to keep the brain ticking over and prevent rapid cognitive regression. Research suggests these brain games may help sharpen your processing speed, planning skills, reaction time, decision-making skills and short-term memory.

Consider a sports star – a basketball, football or netball player. When they are on the court or field, they are alert to their team-mates, the ball and their opponents. It is the same when you are at work. Think of yourself as a work athlete with your brain on alert. When you are developing and building your curiosity muscle, your brain will open up to new ideas and innovative ways of working, problem-solving and seeking out solutions. If you are not curious, new ideas may go straight past you, like the ball on a basketball court. Be alert! How many times has a colleague fixed a problem, identified an issue or come up with a new idea that crossed your mind or seems so obvious, yet you didn't explore it?

Consider athletes when they stop playing the game. How quickly does their body change when it's not being used to the same capacity? It is the same at work – stop being curious and you lose your curiosity.

The biggest benefit of being curious at work is that it will help you to enjoy, even love, your job. Many people I meet leave their jobs because they are bored. Their referees often comment that they started off well, they were conscientious and interested, and then their performance tapered off. Being curious helps you maintain your engagement, motivation, stamina and enjoyment at work. You'll be excited to go to work. Who does not want to feel like that? Being happy takes effort. If you think people are born happy, that is a fallacy that can cost you your own happiness! You have to work at being happy, and having curiosity will assist.

Six curiosity-building tips

1. **Listen intently to understand (not just reply).** Ask questions and more questions. This opens up the creative part of your mind needed for problem-solving.
2. **Be aware of your bias and keep an open mind.** Explore without judging. Be as open to learning from the most junior person in the office as you are the most senior. You can be the student and the teacher at the same time.
3. **Be prepared to have your mind changed.** Genuinely seek to understand, even if your initial thoughts are contrary to what you are being told. Always think: no matter how right you feel you are, what if you are actually wrong?
4. **Read from different sources and varying opinions.** Search out the news from different reporters, journalists and news outlets, even from other countries.
5. **Don't accept everything you're told.** I learned this the hard way. When I first started interviewing, I would never dare ask questions of someone more senior for fear of being disrespectful – even if I didn't understand what they were saying. The problem was, when my boss

or, worse, my client asked me a question concerning the candidate, I didn't have the answer. I learned quickly to ask and ask until I understood. For example, if someone has a degree I haven't heard of, I ask about the subjects and the sort of jobs it will likely lead to, which also assists me in uncovering the candidate's transferable skills. Asking questions indicates you are resourceful, not that you are stupid.

6. **Be an explorer.** Don't label something as boring or think that you already know about it, so you don't explore further. This will close your mind to the topic. If you're not in the mood for something, don't dismiss it. This is your mind encouraging you to stay in your comfort zone – now that is boring!

From the files

A good friend of mine studied marine engineering and worked as an engineer in the navy. When he was looking for a new role, he engaged a recruiter for help. The recruiter was not an engineer, but she was curious about the applicant's field of study, and asked enough questions that she was able to fully understand the candidate's capability. Understanding that my friend's degree was about big machinery, among other things, assisted the recruiter in landing him a job with a mining company – a similar large operation.

My friend changed careers many years later to work as an advisor for an insurance brokering firm. In this job, he helped the firm's clients find the right policy for occupational health and safety within the industry sectors where he had worked – mining, manufacturing and shipping.

This is a great example of both the recruiter and the candidate learning, adjusting, adapting and focusing on the many traits of employability.

TECHNICAL SKILLS

Depending on your chosen field, there might be a range of technical skills required for entry. By technical skills, I mean those skills that relate directly to your ability to do the job. For example, nurses, barristers, teachers and hairdressers all require a level of skills and qualifications to be admitted into their profession.

It's no longer enough to only gain technical skills for entry into your profession, To be truly employable, you must continually work at and sharpen your skills. When I first interview a candidate for a job, I always ask whether their qualifications are up-to-date or need to be renewed in accordance with their industry's requirements. I then ask how they keep up-to-date with their industry's news. Do they subscribe to industry magazines, attend conferences, update their skills by taking courses (online or otherwise), or follow relevant groups on LinkedIn? Do they network with other people within their profession? Do they have a mentor, or mentor others? How familiar are they with industry trends locally and overseas? Do they know who's who and the personnel moves within their industry? Do they have alerts set up on Google for news, movements or even jobs?

My final question is: how would they rate their skills and expertise? A lot of us evolve professionally, according to our areas or interests or where our strengths lie. For example, hairdressers may move towards colouring and away from styling. A recruitment business owner (like me) might find themselves needing to upskill in branding and marketing as opposed to purely recruiting.

Strong, up-to-date technical skills are crucial to keeping you in the game.

PLANNING FOR LEARNING

Your job and career consume more time than most other activities in your life. They are the cornerstones of your existence. You probably work more than you sleep. The happiness you derive from your job and the financial security it provides impact significantly on the rest of your life. Yet how much time do you put into planning and investing in your job or career?

When you're planning your next holiday, you research where to go, what and where to eat, the weather, travel time and mode of transport, health and safety measures, budget needed and more. You spend time becoming familiar with the destination and the options available.

Ask yourself:

- How much time do you spend each year planning your career, job or employability?
- Where do you want to go this year with your job or career?
- What is needed to achieve this goal?
- How familiar are you with the latest courses available?
- What conferences, events or courses are available this year for you to be part of?
- Are you a member of a networking group? If so, how often do you meet? If not, consider forming your own group – start small, and ensure you have set agendas and dates to keep it on track.
- Do you subscribe to any newsletters, blogs or forums related to your industry?
- Do you put aside time once a week or fortnight to research, read and learn?
- Do you have a budget allocated to your continued learning and investment in yourself?

From the files

I have a client who is MD of a global firm. Each January, he plans the family budget, home renovations, children's trips, schooling, sports, holidays and his career.

He puts time aside to consider where he is at, what he wants to achieve – not just for that year, but years out – and thinks about the milestones to set and progression he needs to meet to reach these goals.

As he incorporates this into his yearly planning, his mindset is always 'on it'. His goals and plans for his career evolve because they're front-of-mind with his active involvement.

Great careers, jobs, vocations and employability don't just happen through osmosis, even if you believe that in your case you've 'been lucky'. Reflect on this for a moment. Things may have occurred at a conscious level, like in my client's case, and I bet this learning attribute has also played a big part in your success.

WHAT IF I'M NOT A 'CAREER PERSON'?

You don't have to be highly career-driven to adopt conscious planning. Being employable is not just for career-minded people eager to climb the ladder fast. Everyone who wants to remain employed has to be employable – and that means planning for development.

Employability is a form of insurance for your life.

Let's look at someone who is not career-driven, and is happy clocking on and off from their job. Their priority is spending time with their family or pursuing hobbies and interests outside of work. But what happens if the demand for this person's skill set or the industry they work in disappears? Think about travel consultants, even before COVID-19. As early as 1998, online travel services such as Webjet were established, signalling a move away from the traditional high street travel agent. Think about car manufacturing in Australia. If your priority is to spend quality time with your family, you still need to plan for employability, as your ability to enjoy your downtime will be significantly impacted if you're without an income.

We now accept the fact that learning is a lifelong process of keeping abreast of change. And the most pressing task is to teach people how to learn.

–

PETER DRUCKER

If you are reading the signs, do you just sit there and wait for the inevitable? You would be surprised how many people do. Is it denial, or wishful thinking, or both?

It can be the result of procrastination and fear, too. You need optimism and self-confidence to be courageous and to keep looking ahead to remain employable. Self-confidence and optimism will also assist you to recognise the signs that your job or industry may no longer be secure and take action – that's the critical part.

Instead of remaining immobile, decide to upskill or transition. In the case of travel agents, demand for their face-to-face services has reduced, not disappeared. Their role has evolved. To remain in the industry they need to be the best, which means fine-tuning their skills or upskilling. Alternatively, they could consider transitioning into another job/industry with their transferrable skills: be that customer service skills or knowledge of travel and holiday destinations.

Whether you are career-minded or have other priorities in life, employability and lifelong learning are critical.

Reality check: how thirsty are you for knowledge?

- What was the last new skill or piece of knowledge you acquired at work?
- When was the last time you were curious and asked an 'odd' question?
- In your quest for knowledge, when did you last do work-related research outside of work hours?
- Have you recently witnessed someone else putting forward an idea you also had?
- When using Google, how often do you read different sources?
- How much effort are you willing to expend in learning?

TOP FIVE TAKEAWAYS

1. Everyone can learn. It's good for you and benefits society!
2. If you are not learning, it's not because you lack the ability. Think about what is really holding you back.
3. Build your curiosity by asking questions and being willing to learn.
4. Stocktake your technical skills. Are you as current and up-to-date as those at the top of your field?
5. Put as much work into planning your career as you do your holidays.

2

Dependability

Gain a modest reputation for being unreliable and you will never be asked to do a thing.

–

PAUL THEROUX

I love this attribute. It's high on my list of what to look for when I employ people for my own business. So much of your working life comprises the comings and goings of the people you have worked with, but those who are dependable, even when they leave, stay forever in our lives. (As an aside, I like to think I'm highly dependable!)

A dependable, employable person will be accountable and trustworthy. Of course, they will also be punctual, reliable and honest – these are a given for anyone who values their place in the workforce.

Dependability is your best friend who you've known for many years and can call at any time of the day or night. It's not a fair-weather attribute; it's there no matter what – reliable and rock solid, in good and bad times. Who doesn't want that? That's an attribute to be treasured.

In this chapter we are going to consider:

- the link between dependability and accountability
- how to be dependable under pressure
- the importance of trust
- why employers value dependability
- how being dependable will help you.

DEPENDABLE MEANS ACCOUNTABLE

Being dependable is about being accountable at all times. It doesn't mean being perfect, or never making a mistake. Those things are just not possible – you are a human, not a machine! Being dependable as an employee does mean being consistent in your performance, as well as having a high level of accountability if something goes wrong.

Accountability is how you handle your mistakes and errors. If you are someone who takes ownership for them, you are well on your way to developing the dependability attribute. Your employer won't remember the mistake or issue (well, not for too long, depending upon its magnitude). They will remember that you took responsibility for your own error and your actions, that you learned from the experience and, of course, that you put steps in place to prevent it from happening again.

DEPENDABLE UNDER PRESSURE

Dependability shines brightest when the pressure is on. Being on time for work is important, but that's the base level of being dependable. At its most critical level, dependability is being relied upon and accountable when the chips are down and the pressure is piled on. If you want to be highly employable, be dependable in these circumstances.

We all love working with smart, talented people. It's a joy! When everything is going okay and ticking along, everyone looks good, but when things get tough it's a different story. Ask any employer, business leader or manager – when the pressure is on, dependability counts every time and at every job level. I have worked with highly intelligent, incredibly capable people – members of Mensa, even – but I'd trade the Mensa credential for dependability any day (or have both if I could!).

Dependability is more important than talent.
Dependability is a talent, and it is a talent all can have.
It makes no difference how much ability we possess
if we are not responsible and dependable.

–

FLOYD L. BENNETT

TRUST

Trust is a critical component of being dependable. A trustworthy person is dependable, and a dependable person builds trust by holding themselves accountable. Trust is also a process, not just a feeling, and takes time. Trust in any relationship removes the uncertainty and makes for predictability. When you're dependable and hold yourself accountable, you build trust with your employer and your fellow employees.

Stephen R. Covey, bestselling author of *The 7 Habits of Highly Effective People*, refers to 'the economics of trust'. It's a simple but true formula. Trust affects two outcomes: speed and cost. When there is high trust, speed (efficiency) goes up and cost goes down. Conversely, when trust is low, speed (inefficiency) reduces and there are higher costs.

The following 'From the files' shows how this plays out in recruitment.

From the files

Recruitment is a service industry. We supply the service of sourcing a candidate. When there is high trust with our clients, the process is smooth, efficient and successful. From start to finish, the process takes up to two weeks at the most – there is one shortlist and on average three candidates submitted.

When there is low trust, the process can take over a month – more than double the standard time. The reduced trust means clients feel they need to micromanage the process. They ask to see more résumés as they are sceptical of the selection and benchmarking criteria we use. This requires rework and, in the interim, the original strong candidates submitted have taken other jobs. This leads to more work and a lengthier process, resulting in reduced speed and higher costs. Often, there is no placement, which increases overall costs across the business and misplaced resources, reducing speed to other parts of the business.

How does this relate to your employability? You play a part in creating trust, no matter your position. You could be the chief financial officer or a new graduate. In the recruitment example above, you could be:

- The person who answered when the client called. Were you courteous, professional, well-spoken and efficient, establishing a crucial good first impression?
- The consultant dealing with the client. Were you credible, polished, efficient and professional?
- The accountant at the end of the process. Did you invoice the client correctly and on time?

Everyone and everything is interconnected. When one part shakes, the rest will become more fragile.

According to Covey, trust is the one thing that changes everything. It can make something go from bad to great and vice versa. You create trust at work by being dependable and accountable. I encourage you to flex your dependability muscle wherever and whenever you can, and to do so from the first level of responsibility you take on. Demonstrate your dependability early on and establish mutual trust with your employer.

It is impossible to be dependable without taking responsibility and being trustworthy. Don't blame others or circumstances being 'out of your control'. Instead, become better at self-assessment, reflection and taking on feedback.

WHY EMPLOYERS VALUE DEPENDABILITY

Employers love dependability. When you are dependable, it means your employer trusts you to do your job. Not only that, if something goes wrong, they know it will not be because of carelessness – it will be a genuine mistake. Plus, you will do your best to find a solution, fix it and learn from it.

There are two main reasons employers value your dependability:

1. it gives them peace of mind
2. it's good for business.

Peace of mind

Think about the things in your life that give you peace of mind. Let's consider the car you purchase. In most cases, the number-one criterion for consumers is how reliable the car is. Its reliability gives you peace of mind. Recall a time, even if it was just the once, when your car broke down. Can you remember the sinking feeling, the inconvenience and the hassle and time it took to get it fixed, not to mention the cost? After you've had it repaired, did the thought 'will it start today or break down again' cross your mind? Instead of peace of mind you had concern, worry or even stress.

If you are an employee, you want to be that car that starts each time and doesn't break down (melt down). If anything does happen that prevents you from doing your job, you can be relied upon to have a contingency plan.

Having dependable staff means a business owner, employer or manager can focus on the business. They are not triple-checking or micromanaging. This means they have time to create business plans and strategies for growth and improvement. Their mind is freed up for creative and strategic thinking – all critical parts of what is indeed in their own job description. If you can give your employer time to do this part of their job, they will be forever holding you up as a shining example. Please don't underestimate the value this contribution can be to a business and your boss.

From the files

Years ago, I needed an urgent back operation. It required me to be out of the office for some weeks after the procedure. When it comes to my business, I can apparently be a control freak, making sure our clients and candidates are looked after and receive the best of service. With slight (unfounded) trepidation, I left the care of my clients and candidates in the hands of my team. During my absence, one consultant stood out. She had less than a year's experience, so she was quite junior. However, she excelled.

She put in the effort, extending herself to deliver, ensuring everything was taken care of. It did mean staying back and working harder and longer, but she did it because she knew I was depending on her and to her it was simply the right thing to do. This consultant also had pride in her work and wanted to show me she was capable.

After I recovered, the relationship dynamic between us became stronger. The bank account of trust rose for both of us and that was a wonderful feeling. This consultant went on to become one of the most trusted and high-performing consultants in my team and, even though she has since left my business, we are still in touch regularly (hi, Kerri!).

Good for business

The second reason that employers love employees who are dependable is because they are good for business. If you display the dependable attribute, you create value for the business. As Covey says, value comes from efficiency and low cost, which is linked to trust.

Efficient workplaces don't occur by chance. They're the result of teams of people working together, following systems, applying best practices and displaying positive traits. For a team to perform at its best, each member must be someone the others can count on. All team members must all be dependable.

Your local cafe employs waitstaff. Let's consider how the cafe business is affected by staff members who are not dependable:

- **If a staff member runs late quite regularly:** the cafe is not set up to open on time. Customers won't hang around waiting.
- **Customers start to deem the cafe unreliable:** how do they know they can get their coffee every day at 7 am, in time to catch their train? They try the cafe next door.
- **Staff members call in sick on a too-regular basis:** this causes staff shortages.
- **Team members start to feel one of them has breached trust, and stress levels become visible:** this gives a poor customer experience, as customers can feel the stress. They seek a calmer vibe, so they don't come back.

- **Staff members do not clean the tables adequately:** this gives the perception that staff don't take pride in their workplace, and that there are hygiene issues. The customers go elsewhere.

This loss of business comes down to the lack of dependability of the staff. As a direct result of the staff not being dependable, the business loses customers, sales and profit.

If the staff in this scenario had been dependable, their behaviour would have had the opposite effect. Let's take another look:

- **The staff are never late.** The cafe is always set up and ready to open on time. Customers know this and know that they can rely on getting their daily coffee quickly and early. There is high efficiency due to higher customer retention. This is key for business as you save money by not having to scout for new customers. Customers might even call ahead or order via an app, making it even more efficient.
- **Customers become loyal and tell their friends that the cafe is reliable.** The busier the cafe, the better the prospective customer's perception: 'The coffee and food must be good since it is always busy.'
- **Absenteeism isn't an issue.** The employees trust that when their colleagues call in sick, they are doing so because they don't want to spread germs or be a weak link in the chain, unable to work to full capacity. Customers feel this mutual trust and respect among the staff. The team is high functioning, like a well-oiled machine. Business is slick. Customers like the vibe. Staff from other cafes want to work there.
- **Staff members take pride in cleaning the tables and clearing up quickly and efficiently.** They have pride in their workplace. There are no hygiene issues. Customers can feel comfortable and safe. This means good reviews, tips and repeat business. Win-win!

It doesn't matter what your job is. In this example you might be a barista, kitchen hand or waitperson. It doesn't matter if this is your temporary career choice or whether you are part-time, casual or full-time, you play a part in the efficiency and success of the organisation where you work. Your dependability has a direct impact – always!

HOW BEING DEPENDABLE CAN BE GOOD FOR YOU

Being dependable is not about being self-serving. When you have this mindset, your thoughts and behaviours will always centre on what serves you. There is a time and a place for serving yourself and, in fact, you need to look after yourself, but there is also a time to put other people and causes ahead of your own.

The good news is that if you are dependable and acting in service of the business, *you* will benefit – not just your employer. How? Let's take a look.

It will reduce stress

We have established that being accountable is a critical component of being dependable. What does being accountable at work look like? It is more than simply putting your hand up to say, 'it was me.' This is certainly the first step, however it is also about the 'how and where to from here'.

Say you are running a project and relying on other people's work to meet the deadlines. One person submits their work, but it's incorrect. Their piece of work is critical to meeting your deadlines for the project. You address it with the person and they have two possible responses:

1. 'Oh really? Are you sure? The instructions must not have been clear.' (They are not taking responsibility or being accountable.)
2. 'Oh really? I'm so sorry. Can you please explain what you mean? Oh, now I see. What can I do to fix this for you now?' (They are being accountable and taking responsibility.)

In the second response, the person is seeking solutions to fix the problem immediately and saying afterwards, 'I see how I made this mistake.' Then they move forward, thinking, 'This is how/what I'll do in future.' They're responsible and accountable.

How the person feels in each of these scenarios is vastly different. With the first response, they may feel defensive, and perhaps stressed and pressured. They will feel conflict between themselves and you, the project manager. By blaming the instructions or another person they might even start to feel helpless – that's another level of stress.

In the second scenario, while the person might feel discomfort admitting their mistake, their stress will be reduced in the longer term. They are fixing the issue and they will learn from the mistake. It feels much more productive and less stressful to take responsibility for your own errors. Plus, it is a conduit for positive relationships, which is one of the biggest stress relievers of all.

It will build your trust bank

If you have regularly let someone down, for example by being late, it takes time to regain that trust – significant time, in fact. Think of it like a bank account where interest is applied. The first withdrawal is fine and has minimal impact; the second and third withdrawals are starting to significantly impact the balance. You are earning interest on lower and lower amounts, and you are not making additional deposits to compensate for this.

If you have been late on numerous occasions and you decide that it will never happen again and have made a commitment to change that part of your behaviour, that is great. However, your employer will only know that once they have been shown it repeatedly. They are not privy to what has determined your change of behaviour; they can only witness this from what they see. Consistency is the key.

Let's now consider a staff member who is always on time, never absent, always flexible and, going back to our cafe example, can make shifts at short notice on the occasions when someone else has let the cafe owner down. How do you think this individual is viewed, and how much trust is sitting in their bank account? They are more likely to get better shifts – shifts that work with their other needs and responsibilities, shifts that pay better, and more responsibility so that their job becomes more engaging.

Of course, being punctual is the entry-level requirement of dependability. It's a fundamental requirement. Dependability extends to far greater, more critical areas of your employment.

You won't be micromanaged

Micromanagement kills innovation and creativity and removes the feeling of being in control or having the freedom to make decisions.

We all hate being micromanaged. Here is a secret: a good manager also hates to micromanage – it kills their innovation and creativity as well! If you look at your manager's job description, I can promise it won't include 'micromanagement'. If the style of management you're receiving has shifted, have you considered why?

If you start to miss deadlines, do you think your manager will give you more responsibility? Instead, they are likely to be checking up on you regularly, especially before looming deadlines. You might consider it micromanagement; they consider it plain old management.

The good news is that you can get back on track. Firstly, a good manager will hold their team members accountable. They will give you feedback which you can take on board to change your behaviour.

You can work on your dependability attribute to increase your employability. Try to be self-aware (we look at this is chapter 5). Analyse the situation you are in, be aware of bias and don't be defensive. What behaviours have you displayed or not displayed that have contributed to the situation? Like any formula, if you are part of the equation, adjusting the weighting or contribution levels will change the outcome.

You'll have more freedom and responsibility

When you are dependable, apart from assisting in your employability and professional development, there is another incredible benefit for you. It is what I refer to as the cause-and-effect factor.

When you are dependable, your boss will likely give you more freedom, autonomy and responsibility. If, however, you are not so dependable (as in the examples we looked at above), this won't occur. It will mean your manager is always checking your work, looking over your shoulder or following up. Again, the more time your manager puts into managing you or your projects, the higher the cost and lower the speed as they are taken away from their other responsibilities.

If you are in a situation at present where you are being managed more than you would like, and you would like more autonomy, freedom and responsibility at work, then consider the role you may have played in making this your reality: cause and effect; choice and consequences.

Four habits for dependability

When working on your dependability attribute, consider setting up these habits:

1. complete all tasks not just on time, but early
2. exceed standard levels of work
3. when something goes wrong, analyse what you could have done better – be honest with yourself
4. look to see what else you could be doing to add value and assist your team and manager.

Being conscientious works hand-in-hand with trust, reliability and dependability. Being conscientious requires a level of self-management and self-motivation.

Reality check: how dependable are you?

- Can you recall a time, in any of your jobs, where you have had to work longer hours to finish a task?
- How often do you run late or submit reports past the deadline?
- Does your manager trust you to complete tasks or projects that are known to be difficult?
- When something has gone wrong, how often do you bring in outside variables as reasons and causes rather than looking at your own mistakes?
- When a setback occurs, do you take responsibility for getting things back on track?
- Would you depend on you?

TOP FIVE TAKEAWAYS

1. You can choose to be dependable.
2. Building trust is crucial.
3. Be dependable during times of pressure – not just when it suits you.
4. Be accountable and responsible for your own behaviour and mistakes.
5. Being conscientious, unselfish and self-aware are important parts of being dependable.

3

Resilience

Do not judge me by my successes, judge me by how many times I fell down and got back up again.

–

NELSON MANDELA

Resilience is a must-have for anyone I employ in my business. For me, it means you will keep trying, put the effort in and not give up. You will see adversity and setbacks as 'passing states', and will not be trapped by external unfavourable conditions. Being resilient does not imply that you will endure stress and adversity without any pain, however.

According to psychology experts Jane E. Clarke and Dr John Nicholson, resilience – your capacity to cope with stress and catastrophe – is 'the hottest new topic in psychology, medicine and social sciences'. In their book *Resilience: Bounce Back from Whatever Life Throws at You* they coin the phrase 'resilience quotient', elevating its importance to that of the intelligence quotient (IQ) and emotional intelligence (EQ). In recent times, as the world has been going through a pandemic, most of us have had our resilience tested on both personal and professional levels.

In this chapter, we will look at the importance of resilience for employability. We'll cover:

- how resilience can be acquired
- ways to build your resilience muscle
- finding resilience to stay the course
- emotional versus practical resilience
- bouncing back quickly
- the importance of failure for building resilience.

RESILIENCE CAN BE ACQUIRED

The good news is that resilience is an acquired attribute.

Consider blue cheese. Some would say it's an acquired taste, meaning the more often you eat it, the more likely you are to enjoy it. You are not likely to appreciate a delicious, creamy blue Castello unless you have been exposed to it a few times. Resilience is the same: unless you have had substantial exposure to it, you are unlikely to appreciate the value of resilience. So, be prepared to face challenges that will develop your resilience. One day, you might even enjoy being resilient.

Some people believe resilient people are 'born that way'. Not true! Resilience-building skills can be learned. You do have a choice, and the starting point is refusing to be defined by unpleasant and challenging events and circumstances.

Developing resilience tests you emotionally, psychologically and physically. The lifetime effort required to build resilience will test your limits and boundaries. Resilience is not escapism, nor is it a shield that will stand between you and life. In embracing and accepting it you will ultimately see the full extent of this gift.

Resilience does not present itself in a nice, neat package. Becoming resilient takes you outside of the norm and your comfort zone.

RESILIENCE IN A PANDEMIC

It's fair to say 2020 was a difficult year. It has been referred to as a 'black swan event'. It seemingly came from nowhere and had a once-in-a-generation devastating health, economic and psychological impact.

At the start of the new decade, toasting the new year, my plan for 2020 had been to finally commit to working four days a week to spend more time with my family. That lasted three weeks. As COVID-19 hit, the economy took a dive and so did the business I had founded 10 years ago. Instead of working four days a week, I had to work six or seven and put in 12 to 14-hour-days – for the entire year. And that effort was to keep my office lights dimmed, not even shining at their full capacity.

Many businesses were forced to do the same, if not more. I felt discouraged at times – frightened, emotional, teary. I doubted myself on occasions, but it never occurred to me to give up. I drew heavily on my stores of resilience. However, just because I went through a tough or challenging situation does not make me resilient. The whole world went through COVID-19; does that make everyone in the world resilient? It was how I reacted during and after the event that showed my resilience.

Let's look at some ways you can build resilience.

HOW TO BUILD YOUR RESILIENCE MUSCLE

I am grateful now for experiencing challenging times and situations during my life, although at the time I may not have felt this way. Like tasting blue cheese for the first time, I wanted to spit out these adverse experiences, but I kept going. Some of these challenges were significant – such as working in recruitment during the global financial crisis (GFC), when firms were downsizing and closing, making my job very difficult and emotionally draining.

And, more recently, COVID-19 brought with it a unique situation that governments around the world are still struggling to cope with. Other challenges I've experienced were just trying and consuming of my energy – personal, professional, career obstacles, additional study and so on.

Resilience for me started at a young age. Mine is not a story of hardship or adversity. Resilience does not always have its roots in tough life stories. Everyone's journey is unique and follows a different script.

I spent most of my youth in the country, during a time that was still considered quite 'safe'. We could leave our doors unlocked and windows open, and children could play safely outside. We had freedom and space, we tested boundaries, explored and let our imaginations run wild. When your imagination takes you on a ride, it creates wondrous opportunities and blue-sky moments. If you let yourself dream and be taken over by excitement, you start to believe you can achieve your goals and dreams. This is one way to build resilience: embrace optimism.

Embracing optimism

Optimism is crucial for building resilience. It is the lifeblood of resilient people. It helps them achieve their goals. For them, the idea and thrill of success outweighs the fear of failure.

The excitement and enthusiasm for the opportunity means putting the effort in and applying determination to succeed and not give up.

Seeing the big picture, the upside on the other side of the challenge, will help you push through. If you don't believe there's something on the other side of the struggle, why would you bother? Without optimism, you cannot be highly resilient.

Belief that something larger than us exists drives some people. Research by Brian D. Ostafin and Travis Proulx indicates that there is a connection between meaning in life and resilience to stressors:

those of us whose lives feel meaningful 'experience less stressor-related distress and repetitive negative thinking.'

Chapter 7 provides guidance for working on your optimism attribute.

Setting goals

Setting goals is important in developing your resilience. You can set goals in all areas of your life:

- sports and fitness goals, such as training to run a marathon
- financial goals, such as saving for a car, a holiday or a house deposit
- career goals, where you set goals to work your way up to your dream job.

By setting short-term milestones on the way to your significant goals, you'll feel as though you are chipping away and making progress. You'll enjoy the small wins on the way to your ultimate success. A mixture of short and long-term goals is important in developing the skill set for resilience.

At job interviews, I always ask a potential employee about long-term goal setting or previous goals they have set themselves and achieved. If they did not achieve a goal, I want to know why. I want to understand if it was a (self) saboteur that influenced the outcome or if it was good decision-making (more about this later in the chapter).

Study and overseas experiences

Study of any sort is another way to build your resilience. I'd wager that every single person in the history of the universe who has ever studied has, at some stage, no matter for how brief a time, been tempted to quit. The reasons vary; some are legitimate and warranted, but the majority are not.

Here is a hiring and recruitment secret: one of the reasons employers like to hire people with degrees is not down to the qualification itself. It is because the completion of non-compulsory study demonstrates that important resilience attribute.

Of course, a degree teaches you specific skills and knowledge, but it also tests your ability to work through and achieve a goal. For some people, this will be the first time their resilience is tested. I am never deterred by someone taking longer to complete their degree or studying later in life – I see that as a positive. It shows commitment, tenacity and resilience, as they will often have competing commitments – such as family, work, health or relationship challenges – to juggle while they complete their course of study. All the time, their resilience muscle is being strengthened.

Living overseas is similar. If you have lived and worked overseas, a whole new dynamic of survival will have come into play – especially if the language in that country was not your first language. Living overseas and travelling requires you to adapt to new cultures, customs and people. It pushes you out of your comfort zone. It places you in situations without familiar support mechanisms. You have to start relying more on yourself and less on others – become more self-sufficient and trust yourself.

These are all elements that contribute to the development of resilience.

THE RESILIENCE TO STAY THE COURSE

Be wary of mind games. Do you have a little voice that pops into your head at the hardest and most challenging times, telling you to quit? I call this inner voice your own little saboteur (OLS). It is a trickster; it's not here to help you. It will do a good job of disguising itself as your best friend, only to lead you down the wrong path.

With practice, you'll learn the subtle differences between the helpful voice in your head and the OLS.

Typically, the OLS comes to play at the difficult and challenging times when your resilience is tested the most. It may be at those critical transformational points in your growth and development. You might be well out of your comfort zone, feeling vulnerable and as if you are failing. It might simply seem easier to just quit.

When tempted to quit, make sure you examine your situation and the reasons at the core of your intent. If you are running away because you feel disempowered, you may be creating the opposite effect and erode your self-confidence and self-esteem. However, if you are coming from a place of strength, letting go could be the appropriate course of action.

Of course, the opposite may be true: it may be the time to find the mettle to keep going, to stretch yourself intellectually to see an alternate view or put in additional time to make it work. Seeing the big picture and what it looks like through the other side is critical in determining what course of action to take.

The saboteur may be telling you to quit because your life will be easier, but sometimes the easier option is not the best option or what is good for you. Your emotional intelligence will guide you in determining the right decision. You will find many ways to justify quitting – and, in fact, you will always find more reasons to quit than to stay the course, because that's the OLS's job!

If you're not careful, your OLS can dominate your thinking. Being self-aware will assist you in recognising if negative thinking is becoming an unhealthy pattern. If you are starting to catastrophise situations or events, worrying 'what if' or unreasonably overacting, this may be an indicator.

If this has become your reality, it is hard to distinguish between what is likely to happen and what you are making up in your head. I suggest having a sounding board to talk to: someone who will be honest with you, so maybe not your mum or best friend. Choose someone who will give you the truth, even if it's not what you want to hear. Remember to thank them!

EMOTIONAL VERSUS PRACTICAL RESILIENCE

Studies show that there are negative and positive forms of coping resilience:

- **Negative coping resilience** is when you bury or avoid a problem, or depend excessively upon others to solve the problem for you.
- **Positive coping resilience** comprises two alternatives:
  1. Problem-focused coping: when you deal with characteristics of the situation.
  2. Emotional-focused coping: when you deal with the emotional effects of stress provoked by the situation.

Dealing with emotions may be the only realistic option when the situation is outside your control (for example, when an emergency response worker is unable to save a patient).

Problem-focused coping is helped by having a good job-related knowledge base: for example, when high workload is an issue, knowing what's urgent and what can wait can help a worker prioritise effectively and feel less overwhelmed.

Like working any muscle, you need to feel the pain to know you're growing. True resilience does not mean you never get discouraged. If you never encounter a painful struggle, you never get to discover your resilience. This is why experiencing pain is almost universal among the resilient.

BOUNCING BACK QUICKLY

Resilience is not just weathering the storm. If you just weather the storm you will be worn out, fatigued, burnt out and drained. This is often the misconception about resilience. It is not about just making it through, it's about *how* you make it through.

Resilience is your coping ability and bounce-back factor. It's your ability to overcome a challenge and move forward with strength. Highly resilient people find a way to change course, emotionally heal and continue moving towards their goals.

According to author and organisational psychologist Adam Grant, resilience is 'the speed and strength of your response to adversity. So, when you encounter a difficulty, a hardship, a challenge, how quickly and how effectively are you able to marshal strength and either overcome that challenge or persevere in the face of it?' Dr Ellen Hendriksen sees resilience as adapting and responding positively to stress and misfortune – and doing so quickly.

Stress doesn't have to be traumatic or tragic. Every day, you are exposed to tiny challenges that require some 'micro resilience': not losing your cool in traffic, or when your partner's running late (or your laptop freezes mid-book-writing at 5 am and you haven't saved your changes!).

It's the way you respond and how long it takes you get back to 'normal' again that is important. (It did take an hour-long dog walk for me to regain my composure after the laptop freeze, I admit it!)

Consider a setback at work. The longer you allow yourself to stay in the static situation and not move forward, the less productive you and your team will be. When you are highly resilient, you are dependable (your employer knows you will move forward) and you'll be optimistic (you'll see the way forward, the upside, blue skies). Employees who are resilient are highly employable. Resilient employees do not let themselves become overwhelmed with unnecessary emotions. They preserve their energy and move to solutions.

At the same time, resilience isn't about masking your pain, being tough and pretending everything is great. Feeling emotional and displaying vulnerability is healthy for you and lets you know you are in the throes of developing your resilience.

Resilience is not as simple as turning a switch on and off. It requires strengthening and testing on a regular basis – daily, even, if we refer to our micro-resilience sessions earlier. You can find your challenges and they do not all have to be hard and difficult. Some of them will be fun, if you choose it to be that way.

DOES RESILIENCE HAVE A DARK SIDE?

It's fine to talk about bouncing back, but experts acknowledge that resilience has its negative or 'shadow' side too.

Dr Adam Fraser is one of these experts. He talks about the dark side of resilience:

> *People today are not lacking resilience, they are lacking the permission to take care of themselves, the ability to recover and refresh and the capacity to get past guilt so that they can embed rituals that allow them to do things that fill up their tanks.*

He encourages you to ask whether you need more resilience, or need recovery and self compassion. You need to listen carefully to the messaging you are receiving and what you are believing.

FAILURE IS GOOD

Unfortunately, you can't build resilience on success alone. It takes failure to build your inner strength. A life of unbroken success or continuous happiness does not test us (nor does it exist). If you are untested, then you are unprepared for what might come.

When failure starts, that's when the hardest resilience lesson begins. What if you didn't complete your degree? It may not be considered a failure, but for the purpose of what we are analysing, it's a learning opportunity. You are the only person who will know if, really, you should have completed your degree and whether you could have stuck at it. You will know if you quit for the right reasons or not. More importantly, how are you feeling about it now? Not completing your degree will not define you. It's how you move forward that counts.

Be your own best friend by building your self-awareness (chapter 5) – analyse and learn from your mistakes.

If you want to achieve something great in life, you need resilience, no matter what you are working towards. A degree is one small aspect. Recent research shows people with early career setbacks and near misses systematically outperform those with narrow wins in the longer run.

Reality check: how resilient are you?

- Can you recall a challenging period that required you to keep going and work through?
- What is a long-term goal you set for yourself and achieved? What challenges did you experience along the way?
- What is your proudest work achievement?
- When was the last time you stopped yourself from having an emotional reaction? How did you feel afterwards?
- What is the difference between your positive inner voice and your saboteur?

TOP FIVE TAKEAWAYS

1. Resilience is an acquired attribute.
2. You can build your resilience muscle.
3. If there is a choice to quit or keep going – always try not to quit.
4. See the bigger picture and be optimistic.
5. Failure is your opportunity to learn.

4

Interpersonal nous

If your emotional abilities aren't in hand,
if you don't have self-awareness, if you are not
able to manage your distressing moments,
if you can't have empathy and can't have effective
relationships, then no matter how smart you are,
you are not going to get very far.

–

DANIEL GOLEMAN

Your interpersonal nous is how well you relate to people. It influences how people feel about you and respond to you in return. We've all worked with someone who is a natural relationship-builder. They seem to get on well with everyone, they seek out opportunities for collaboration, they're assertive without being pushy, and they seem to understand the nuances of conflict and be able to resolve it intuitively. They are the person everyone wants to work with.

Employers love to hire people who have a natural gift for building strong interpersonal relationships. That's because these people make the working environment better and their manager's life easy! There's no need to worry about drama or conflict when you have someone with strong interpersonal skills on your team. You know they will always bring the team together and motivate those around them.

The good news is, like all the other attributes, your interpersonal nous can be learned.

This chapter will help you become familiar with how people with great interpersonal nous operate. As a starting point, typically they are strong communicators and naturally build relationships with others. We'll look at:

- how interpersonal nous affects your employability
- types of interpersonal communication
- active listening
- two-way communication
- nonverbal cues, tone and demeanour
- setting boundaries.

HOW GREAT INTERPERSONAL NOUS MAKES YOU MORE EMPLOYABLE

If resilience is blue cheese, interpersonal nous is the icing on the cake. It makes everything taste so much better. Indulgent? Not if you want to feel connected to people, feel fulfilled, have a sense of belonging and be able to see yourself accurately through other people's eyes.

You probably spend more time communicating with people at work than you do with your friends and family. If you can't relate to people successfully and meaningfully, you may be doomed to endure a lonely and uninspiring working life.

Just as icing improves the cake's appearance, so does your ability to communicate well with people make you more attractive to be around. Icing also provides a protective coating around the cake, just like strong interpersonal skills will protect you on your career path. Icing can transform a cake from edible to scrumptious, and your interpersonal skills, in conjunction with your other attributes, will make you always and forever employable.

In a professional environment, when you have good interpersonal skills you interact well as a team member, whether as a manager or at peer level. You win over stakeholders, suppliers and customers. You have strong relationship-building skills and are able to influence, negotiate and cooperate.

Communication is the foundation of strong interpersonal skills – it is where you make magic happen. Good communication skills can improve your relationships by helping you to understand others and be understood. Communication is where you can turn bad to great. Conversely, bad communication can cause a disaster.

Most misunderstandings are a result of poor communication – not understanding, or wanting to understand, what the person is really saying or trying to say. You may think everyone speaks the same language at work, but often people's communication styles are very different.

I am not referring to cryptic industry terminology or acronyms. I am referring to frames of reference, biases, all the components that make you who you are – even before you express yourself. Many people take good communication for granted, yet it is an exceptional skill to have in your armoury.

Good communication can take a lifetime to master. It's an ever-evolving skill. I doubt anyone can claim to have learned all they need to know about communication. Navigating the ideas, opinions and emotions you carry and hope to pass on to others clearly and transparently is a fine art that can be learned and continually improved.

As with other skills, if you don't use your communication skills, you will lose them!

TYPES OF INTERPERSONAL COMMUNICATION

Communication is not only about speaking and writing. It is significantly more complex, making it so beautifully confusing and delicate at the same time.

Communication can be:

- listening
- understanding
- taking subtle cues
- self-awareness
- nonverbal.

No matter your role or position in the company, from the most junior to the most senior, skilled communication can be your secret weapon. Think of it as your seventh sense!

From the files

While I was living in Japan I took a short holiday to the UK. I went to a shoe shop in London and found a gorgeous pair of shoes. I asked for my size and the shop assistant said they did not have them in stock. I could tell she was not telling the truth – my Japanese experience helped me in building the skills to read the signs and cues, not just the words. I could tell the shop assistant simply could not be bothered to go and look for the shoe in my size. So, I politely asked if perhaps she could double-check in the storeroom for me. She did, and what do you know? She returned with the shoes in my size. I walked out of the shop with my glorious, precious trophy (my feet were too big to buy nice shoes in Japan!) and a sense of wonder and incredulity.

I have never forgotten that experience and the realisation that I had learned a new skill. It gave me more confidence in my ability to read people and tell whether or not they were being honest. This skill has helped me countless times during my career in recruitment, and in my personal life.

LISTENING: THE KEY TO INTERPERSONAL HARMONY

Communication is about listening. Listening is not easy and is not the same as hearing.

When you listen properly, you understand deeply and comprehend the other person's meaning. You do not only hear the sound, you also hear the message. Listening requires effort and patience.

Listening and understanding leads to light-bulb moments, where you have a breakthrough of clarity and can see the other person's view. When this happens, the communication becomes fluid and the very best negotiations can occur. Magic!

When you are deep in a discussion or argument, exchanging views and information, negotiating, disagreeing – whatever it may be – you may think you understand well before you really do. You might think you know what the issue is or what the speaker is trying to say, and you're too quick to jump the gun, cut the person off and offer up your ideas, solutions and agenda. This is not effective listening and it indicates poor communication skills.

Following your brain script while someone is talking will prevent you from taking in their information and opinions. Your enthusiasm to get to the crux of the situation, solve the problem or contribute your point of view may make the other person feel unheard, misunderstood, disrespected, frustrated and, in some cases, dismissed. From here, they are likely to shut down and stop being receptive to you.

Mastering the ability to quieten the dialogue in your head while listening is crucial. One tool that can help with this is active listening.

Active listening is where you take time to listen all the way through the other person's message, paying careful attention so that you pick up the subtle reasonings and undisclosed messages. It is the practice of fully concentrating on what is being said, listening with all senses.

When you're listening actively, you can look for 'anchor' or 'key' words that tell you everything you need to know. They might stand out, because they are incongruent with the rest of the message. They are words at the root of the issue and are usually emotional, and they will be repeated throughout the person's message.

For example, I worked with an EA who, when I thanked her for doing a good job, would often say, 'Oh, thank you – I guess it is just because I'm caring.' Her motivator was to be seen as kind and caring beyond everything else.

When I'm interviewing someone who has a strong sense of their own authority or power but doesn't want to be overt in saying so, words such as 'senior', 'managed' or the frequent use of 'I' instead of 'we' often give them away.

There are a few ways to ensure you are listening actively, including taking notes, asking questions and repeating back your understanding of the situation. We do this at EST10 when we're taking job briefs. However, the note-taking must be more than just writing down information; it should be a mental road map with prompts to ask questions, either throughout or at the end. This method assists with your engagement and helps your memory. Be aware of any bias you have, and try to withhold advice, suggestions, judgement and solutions while you're listening.

TWO-WAY COMMUNICATION

Communication goes two ways. The way you speak to others has a direct influence on the way they will reply.

Think of a scenario where someone appears to be aggressive. They raise their voice and say, 'Have you submitted the report?' You will inevitably feel attacked and on edge. Most people will feel intent on defending their position. Depending on your personality, you may become aggressive in return, withdraw or become paralysed and unable to respond.

In these situations, where both parties are operating in this manner, there will be no resolution or amicable outcome.

Instead, imagine a different scenario. A person comes into the room and asks, 'Excuse me, are you free for a few minutes?', or 'Is now a good time?' Then they ask, 'Can you help me understand something? Head office has just called to say they haven't received the report. Are you across how that occurred?'

My tip when communicating a potentially difficult or sensitive message – in email or verbally – is to always 'set the scene'. Have neutral grounds and disarm any potential aggressive response. You can do this by making it clear from the very beginning that the other person has no reason to be concerned or protective, which will prevent them from becoming defensive. In communications, it is often not what you say but how you say it (your tone) that matters.

> **A skilled communicator can quickly defuse a situation by changing the tone, pace, pitch and timing of the conversation.**

Always give the other party the option to delay the discussion if it isn't the right time for them. This also gives both parties time to calm down, detach for a moment and adjust the tone and pace of the conversation. The calmer you are, the better you will be able to listen, understand and comprehend.

Ask questions and more questions to understand a situation and the other person's viewpoint. The more questions you ask, the better placed you will be to find common ground. You will gain knowledge, and the other party will feel heard and may even start to see another side by virtue of the questions you are asking.

PICKING UP NONVERBAL CUES

Recognising and understanding nonverbal cues helps you to be a great communicator and understand people better. Many of us interpret these nonverbal signs incorrectly, based on our own projections and frames of reference, which can lead us to make the wrong assumptions. Make sure you know yourself well and be aware of your biases.

Many of us are not even good at reading the signs of those close to us. How often have you been shocked or surprised to hear of someone leaving their job 'without giving any clue'? And what about romantic partners and children? Their behaviours may seemingly have come out of the blue, but were you really paying attention?

To pick up on nonverbal skills, you must be a great observer. Like many other traits we discuss in this book, this can be learned and practised.

Let's take a look at some of the common nonverbal cues and how you can become aware of them in your own communication.

Body language

Body language is one aspect of nonverbal communication – and it's an important one. Verbal language is perceived by the cerebral cortex, the most highly developed part of the brain. Body language, on the other hand, is perceived by the limbic system, a more primitive system that governs emotions, mood, pain and pleasure. Body language bypasses your conscious processing centre, giving you an innate understanding of the situation without the person saying a word.

Let's look at some examples of body language and what these might be trying to communicate:

- **Handshake:** a firm handshake shows confidence, interest and respect. However, a crushing handshake – especially from a man – is not always appreciated. It can be interpreted as bullying or intimidation.
- **Eye contact:** I look for direct eye contact. It used to be considered that someone had something to hide if they did not connect with their eyes, but I have noticed that with so much of our communication being digital these days, many people have lost the habit of good direct eye contact. However, many people will still interpret poor eye contact as a lack of confidence, especially in a one-on-one situation. This can be a significant problem when it comes to the very attributes we are discussing now: interpersonal skills and communication. Working on building your self-confidence will assist.
- **Leaning in:** I love seeing this. It shows eagerness, interest and intent.
- **Nodding:** this indicates listening.
- **Smiling:** again, this enforces that the person is listening and understanding – if it's the right kind of smile, that is! Not all smiles are good smiles. A forced smile – or what we call in our office the 'nice nasty' – is something to look out for. It's pretty easy to detect this smile, as the eyes will not follow. Eyes sparkle when a smile is genuine.
- **Fidgeting:** this can be a sign of nerves, or boredom. A boredom fidget is usually a slower fidget.
- **Leaning back:** this shows a person is potentially not interested or has switched off.

These are just a few simple signs to look out for. Of course, there are also some neurological conditions that can affect people's body language, and these should be taken into consideration.

From the files

In some cultures, direct eye contact is frowned upon. When I worked in Japan, my direct eye contact by virtue of my Western culture was not a good thing – it was seen as rude, even impertinent.

The Japanese used to say *me ga warui*, literally translated as 'bad eyes', closely followed by *kowai!*, meaning 'scary', because of my eye contact. I quickly learned that to look directly at someone in Japanese culture is a sign of disrespect and aggression.

During my time in Japan, I became so used to avoiding eye contact and bowing automatically to everything to show my respect that I had to work hard to adjust on my return home. I distinctly recall bowing to taxis – the car, not necessarily the driver – when they stopped at traffic to let me cross the road, because that is what you do in Japan.

This is a good example of how misunderstandings can occur and it shows the importance of knowing your own bias and frame of reference.

If you were communicating with someone from Japan who was avoiding eye contact and you didn't know that this was part of their culture, you might think they were being disrespectful and hiding something, when in fact they were showing you the utmost respect.

You need to seek to understand first before judging and using your own frame of reference as the holy grail.

Tone of voice and demeanour

Tone of voice is one of my personal works in progress (WIPs). In the past, I was given regular feedback that when I was in the heat of the moment, my tone wasn't good – it conveyed that I was dismissive, arrogant or condescending. I shudder to think how I was being perceived in the early days of my career. I worked on this a lot. I still slip up on occasion, but I usually catch myself quickly. When I find myself making this communication mistake, I apologise immediately and switch to the right tone.

Another unhelpful way I tend to use my tone is when I am focused on a problem or issue. I enjoy numbers, spreadsheets and writing and like to work on these tasks in peace and quiet with no disruptions – not just because it helps me to focus properly, but because I am enjoying myself! In such situations I have been known to let my guard and awareness down when answering someone's question. I sometimes answer with a particular tone, and no doubt my body language and facial expression matches what I am really saying, which is, 'I am so busy, I'm trying hard to focus and you are bothering me.' This leads the poor person who has interrupted me to think, 'I'm not important,' or 'She has no time for this, best I don't approach her.' Given I have always wanted to be an approachable manager, this behaviour sends the wrong message and is incongruent with my intent.

Your intent might not be to be dismissive, but if you can learn to recognise the potential impact or hurt, and rectify it, it will undoubtedly assist your communication.

No matter your level at work, accepting responsibility and apologising when your tone is unprofessional is important. Courageous leaders don't make excuses, they apologise. When they apologise, they are also showing humility. Humble leaders understand that they are not always the smartest person in every room – they don't need to be. They encourage others to speak up, respect differences of opinion and champion the best ideas.

Facial expressions

Your facial expressions fall into the same category as your tone – they say a lot! Eyebrow-raising, eye-rolling, widening eyes, narrowing eyes, nose scrunching, tilting head, teeth grinding, grimacing – all of these communicate a message that perhaps you do not want disclosed.

Your facial expressions can be hard to detect because they are part of your demeanour and, obviously, you are not usually able to see your own face when you're communicating with others. To find out how your facial expressions might come across, I have two suggestions: ask someone you trust or video yourself.

When you see a recording of yourself, you may be pleasantly surprised – your facial expressions may not be as extreme as you feared. However, when I tried this exercise I was mortified to see my own facial expressions, and I have worked on them ever since. I had no idea that I chewed my cheek, for example, or that I raised my eyes upwards, or that my nose did this weird witch-like thing when I focused on talking to someone. It was disconcerting.

When you say one thing and your facial expression says something different, you are delivering mixed messages and confusing the recipient. This inconsistent messaging will cause distrust – maybe not at a conscious level, but it will stop you from developing the strongest possible connections and relationships.

From the files

This is a scenario I have witnessed on so many occasions. You may recognise a similar situation in your own work environment.

Paul, a senior manager, asked another equally senior colleague, Mary, if she would like to work on a project together. Paul needed Mary's input and expertise to pull off the project, but Mary has been known to be a little disagreeable at times.

Paul said, 'Mary, would you like to work with me on this project? I've been asked by our MD to pull a team together. The client is new, and it will be important for the company.'

Mary responded, 'Sure, I'd be happy to head it up.'

Paul then told the MD that Mary was keen to work on the project. However, he failed to recognise the subtle clue in Mary's wording that illustrates her true feelings about the situation.

Mary was not keen to *work* on the project; she was keen to *head it up*. What she really said was, 'I want to control this project.' In this situation, the communication from both parties was lacking transparency.

As a seasoned communicator and listener, I could tell what Mary was communicating through her keyword cues. However, because Paul was apprehensive about approaching Mary, expecting her to be snappy, he wasn't able to view the situation or Mary's response with clarity. He only saw what he wanted to see: he was relieved that Mary had agreed to take part, and she didn't display an adverse reaction. His frame of reference said to him, 'Mary is happy to help with my project.'

I'm sure you can imagine how Paul's project progressed!

THE IMPORTANCE OF BOUNDARIES

Having strong boundaries in place is important for your interpersonal relationships. Boundaries tell others how you expect to be treated. They are rules, sometimes unspoken, about what you feel is acceptable in terms of others' behaviour towards you.

Your boundaries will be tested often – sometimes repeatedly by the same people – so it's important you remain strong in your boundaries and keep reinforcing how you expect to be treated.

If you're new to setting boundaries, the first time you put them into place may feel very uncomfortable. They will be easier to enforce with practice. Of course, it is far better to have boundaries in place from the beginning rather than trying to set them later, when you have perhaps already communicated that you're okay with being treated in a certain manner.

Boundaries are hard work, particularly for those who like pleasing others, but they are worth it for the advantages they bring.

Once you have set your boundaries you need to review them often. Situations and circumstances may alter them, so make sure that you have the right line marked.

To build strong relationships it's also important to respect others' boundaries. If someone communicates one of their boundaries, either verbally or through body language, take them seriously and act on their request. If you have good boundaries for yourself, you will typically also be respectful of other people and know what is and isn't appropriate, lessening the likelihood of finding yourself in uncomfortable situations.

It's human nature to push boundaries, so regular review of them is necessary.

***

Interpersonal nous is incredibly powerful in all its different formats and it can make or break situations and relationships. A competent, confident communicator who is willing to keep working to improve their interpersonal nous is an asset to any employer.

Reality check: how strong is your interpersonal nous?

- Can you think of a time when you have been able to influence someone to come around to your way of thinking?
- Can you think of a time when you have had your mind changed to another person's way of thinking?
- When was the last time you apologised – genuinely?
- How comfortable are you in saying 'no' and putting appropriate boundaries in place?
- How often have you 'seen' your own body language when speaking with someone?
- How often are you able to hear someone's whole story without interrupting or cutting them short?

TOP FIVE TAKEAWAYS

1. Communication is the foundation of strong interpersonal skills. Good communication skills can improve your relationships by helping you understand others and be understood.
2. Listening is key to deep two-way communication.
3. Beware of your subconscious messaging – what are you communicating that you would rather keep private?
4. Constantly check yourself for your tone and body language.
5. Boundaries are critical to building strong relationships.

5

Self-awareness

To know yourself, you must sacrifice the illusion that you already do.

–

VIRONIKA TUGALEVA

Ever since emotional intelligence (EQ) entered the lexicon of our everyday working lives, self-awareness has become mainstream, its relevance and prominence increasing. EQ, the ability to recognise and understand your emotions and how they affect people around you, is a key factor in being self-aware. Assessing EQ through interview questions, tests, role-plays and more has become everyday practice in the recruitment world, and it's an essential element of employability.

In this chapter, we'll take a look at self-awareness and why it's so essential to your employability. We'll discuss:

- the importance of seeking out feedback
- cultivating self-reflection
- the Johari window technique for self-understanding.

DO YOU BELIEVE YOU ARE SELF-AWARE?

Organisational psychologist Tasha Eurich says self-awareness – knowing who you are and how you're seen – is important for job performance, career success and leadership effectiveness. However, she says, it's in short supply at work. Her research found that even though most people *believe* they are self-aware, self-awareness is a truly rare quality: 'We estimate that only 10 to 15 per cent of the people we studied actually fit the criteria.'

Eurich says that 'experience and power can hinder self-awareness' – that is, we don't always learn from our mistakes. In fact, seeing ourselves as experienced can 'keep us from doing our homework, seeking disconfirming evidence, and questioning our assumptions.'

In her book *Insight: The Power of Self-Awareness in a Self-Deluded World*, Eurich notes that self-awareness is the meta-skill of the 21st century – the foundation for high performance, smart choices and lasting relationships. Unfortunately, we are remarkably poor judges of ourselves and how we come across, she says.

All this leads to the vital importance of developing your self-awareness. Knowing yourself will help you navigate your workplace and life in general. It will aid you in having greater input and control over the outcomes at work, and improve your happiness. Self-awareness is the best gift you can give yourself. And, because so few people are self-aware, possessing this attribute is a great way to set yourself apart in the employability stakes.

Working on your self-awareness can be hard, but it's also extremely rewarding. It is a fascinating exercise of self-discovery. Why would you not want to know who you really are, and how you are being perceived? From there, your perception of others and how you relate to them will help you with sometimes very uncomfortable and complex relationships.

The more you understand yourself and develop your self-awareness, the higher your EQ. In fact, without self-awareness there *is* no EQ, since self-awareness is one of EQ's four domains, as defined by psychologist and journalist Daniel Goleman (see figure 5.1).

Figure 5.1: The four domains of EQ

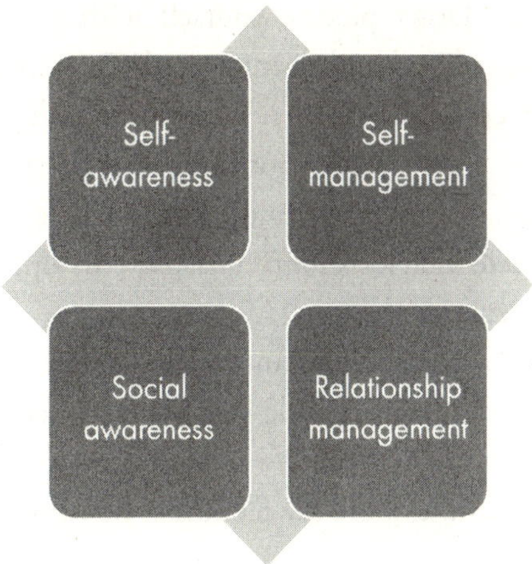

Source: Adapted from Goleman, D 2005, *Emotional Intelligence: Why It Can Matter More Than IQ*, Bantam.

SEEKING OUT FEEDBACK

So, how do you go about developing your self-awareness? This is where feedback is your number-one friend. Feedback is important in cultivating many of the 7 attributes. I believe welcoming feedback is key to being employable. Feedback is critical not just for your self-awareness, but for your learning and adapting. If you are fortunate enough to receive some feedback, think of it as a gift that is helping you become the very best version of yourself.

Feedback is often the missing link in communication. Providing and requesting feedback is a great way to make sure what you are communicating is understood and agreed upon. It shows a level of understanding and reflection; for without reflection, you can't know if the person understood what you were trying to impart.

How open to feedback are you? Are you comfortable in asking for feedback? Do you dread receiving feedback, or simply can't wait to hear it?

Be open to feedback – think of yourself with arms wide open, welcoming it in. Don't picture yourself with your arms crossed across your body, closed and disinterested. To cultivate self awareness you need feedback, and you need to want feedback. Seek it out.

In situations where you're not able to request feedback, self-reflection is key. You need to understand, analyse and reflect on what has occurred, then look for trends, patterns and commonalties. This is self-awareness.

Do not turn a blind eye to an uncomfortable situation. Don't fear or mistrust the person giving you the feedback, imagining the worst possible words that will flow towards you. Don't be ignorant; instead, be brave and explore the feedback. Be curious – think back to chapter 1!

Sensory and direct feedback

There are two types of feedback: sensory and direct. Both require you to participate actively.

Sensory feedback is when you pick up on signs, signals and subtle (and not-so-subtle) cues people are giving you. If you are lucky enough to have heightened self-awareness and well-developed EQ, then you will receive feedback at a sensory level daily, in every encounter. I wrote about humans being receptors in the 'curiosity' section of chapter 1. Are your sensors on, or are they on silent mode and ignoring all cues? If you are open to receiving it, sensory feedback is formidable – you are receiving it from people who are likely unaware they are giving it to you and probably would not be comfortable in letting you know. Their unconscious messaging and body language have delivered these messages to you, but only if your receptors are tuned in and turned on!

Direct feedback is usually given verbally, sometimes written. My preference is always verbal, but circumstances sometimes necessitate written. Verbal feedback could be given in the heat of the moment, which usually means it's reactive, which is not ideal as it incorporates other inflections that undermine the intended message. However, even then, you can garnish some truths (feedback) if you look for it and are brave enough!

When a colleague tells me they are fearful of feedback, I ask them, 'If the feedback were true, wouldn't you want to know?' If the feedback is true and you do not like it, at least you have a chance now to change your behaviour – if you desire and choose to.

Patterns and trends

To find truths from feedback, look for some sort of sequence, pattern or trend. Initially, you will consider isolated comments and signs as random, but when there is a repetition and pattern, you'll see there is an overarching meaning you may need to take on board. Even if you take away only 2 per cent of the feedback, this will go a long way towards a deeper understanding of yourself.

Look for a common word, phrase or expression that might be used in describing you, your communication or style. For me, as I revealed in chapter 4, it was my tone. No matter the circumstances – whether it was a heat-of-the-moment argument or a civilised conversation – that word came to light. While I was disappointed when I realised my tone was an issue, I was pleased to be aware of it. I now treat every one of these pieces of feedback and awareness moments as a gift. I would rather know how I am being perceived and choose whether to change.

With self-awareness, the most crucial thing is to notice the congruency. To be fully self-aware is to achieve perfect alignment between the way you see yourself and how others see you. This may not be something you can attain easily, but you can try to come as close as possible.

Asking for and receiving feedback

In a work environment, feedback is usually delivered by your manager or mentor or, if you are fortunate enough, a colleague. It often comes up during the performance review process.

If your workplace is not one where feedback is a usual part of the culture, you'll need to cultivate a feedback habit yourself by asking for it from trusted colleagues. Remember, the better you are at receiving feedback, the more honest and significant the feedback you receive is likely to be. When people are open to feedback, the giver is inspired rather than inhibited, which makes the input more constructive, honest, profound and significant and, therefore, even more valuable.

If you ask for feedback and you are genuine about knowing the full facts and truth, then you need to be gracious in receiving it – even if you do not like what you have heard or you disagree. If you strongly disagree, ask for examples until you can see or understand. Alternatively, ask for time to consider and revisit in a week.

Remember, what makes feedback so good is your chance to reflect upon it properly, which is a crucial part of the development of self-awareness. You will be surprised what can come to you in a silent moment.

If you are up for it, ask someone else you trust – a friend or partner – for their opinion. Please recognise that if someone cares about you, it is not easy to provide candid feedback, so it is extra important to be gracious and thankful. This will make it easy for them to continue to provide honest feedback.

Be careful about who you ask for feedback. What you want and need is honest feedback from another's perspective, not just praise that you like hearing. Receiving feedback intended to please sometimes has its purpose, but hearing only what you want to hear isn't helpful. You feel alive when you hear the truth, no matter how unpleasant (or even ugly) it may be. Asking for feedback when you're only expecting praise is like opening a present you've chosen yourself and pretending to be surprised. No-one likes having to fake excitement about a 'surprise' present!

It is not easy to receive feedback – in fact, it can be really hard! At times, honest feedback can affect your self-esteem and ego, and you can find yourself becoming defensive. Because asking for and receiving feedback isn't easy, people opt out; but then they miss out on the learning opportunities it can bring.

If you are determined to begin asking for feedback, just keep asking no matter how hard it is. Do not turn back. Your resilience, stamina and self-confidence from addressing the feedback will assist you in sticking with it!

From the files

Early in my career, I was fortunate enough to have the very best of bosses. Chris was not afraid to provide feedback delivered in a manner that was all about supporting me and providing a safe environment for me to receive it.

This was the first time I was made aware of areas to improve, the perception of others and my own blind spots. As it was 360-degree feedback, colleagues, peers and team members provided their feedback and perceptions. I was 30-something, had been promoted rapidly and thought I was a very good performer.

The feedback I received was devastating. I cried. I recall compiling a hit list in my head of who said what and how I intended to act out my revenge. (Not my proudest moment.)

My boss was incredibly supportive and insightful. I recall her saying, 'If you do not respect the people who have provided the feedback, why do you care what they say?' I did respect these people, though. I did not always like them – it was a competitive sales environment – but it mattered to me what they thought.

I needed a couple of weeks to reconcile what my boss had said. I let myself be open to hearing the comments – really hearing what was being said and allowing myself to be wounded (for that is what it felt like). And then I saw some validity and I decided to change. It required a lot of effort and constant awareness. I felt vulnerable on occasions, but I learned that it is normal to feel that way when you are working on parts of yourself that you want to improve or change. I was well out of my comfort zone – exposed, even – but the experience taught me that being in my comfort zone was of no benefit if I was serious about my career and development. It also taught me you need courage to change, and from courage, you embrace your vulnerability as a sign of strength, not weakness.

The caveat here is I had a great manager who made my landing softer because of the trust levels already built. My wish is that everyone, at one time in their career, can experience working for a boss like this.

Even of you don't have this opportunity, you can still seek out feedback, sift through what is relevant and apply what is needed. Get comfortable being out of your comfort zone.

Feedback helps you to learn. If it's powerful enough, it will help you to learn quickly. The moment you embrace this mindset, your life will become so much better.

SELF-REFLECTION

Self-reflection is the process of taking the time to reflect and consider your behaviours and reactions to certain situations. The workplace can be a pressured environment that can sometimes trigger stress, fatigue and frustration. According to leadership expert Jennifer Porter, 'Reflection gives the brain an opportunity to pause amidst the chaos, untangle and sort through observations and experiences, consider multiple possible interpretations, and create meaning.'

Reflection helps you to uncover how you feel in any given situation, so you can work out whether or not your behaviour is consistent with your feelings. I always like to explore those feelings – it taps into your subconscious and can assist in peeling back the layers to understand yourself better. When you have a heightened awareness of your innermost thoughts, actions and behaviours, you can choose to make the changes in your life that you want. Your vista is clear and broad, and you can ask yourself whether your thoughts and behaviours are working in your best interests. If the answer is 'no', you will then have the chance to work on them.

Here is the other thing with self-reflection: to hone the skill, you can't just keep it to yourself; you have to test your hypotheses. You need a mentor or a trusted source to ask for opinions and thoughts. I find I can still slip up by not realising my biases and letting the insecure part of my psyche take over. Previously I was not even aware this was happening. Now I am aware I religiously test whether my own triggers are sabotaging me.

Five tips for cultivating self-reflection

1. **Try free-association journalling.** Set a timer for five minutes and write whatever comes into your head. This practice of checking in with yourself can be a helpful way to uncover any lurking issues that are bothering you, so you can take action.

2. **Choose a time that suits you.** If you're a morning person, there isn't much point in trying to self-reflect in the evening when your brain is exhausted and you're likely to catastrophise.

3. **Assess your self-talk mindfully.** Is your first thought about every situation negative? Do you obsess over 'nothing'? Do you believe that you are the cause of every misunderstanding? Ponder this.
4. **Analyse the situation and hold yourself accountable, no matter what happened.** Look for what you could have done better, even if the situation is not your fault or responsibility. The purpose of this tip is to stretch your awareness.
5. **Create a quiet space.** I know, this might be easier said than done but even 10 minutes of silence in the car may be enough for you to check in with yourself.

THE JOHARI WINDOW

Remember Chris, the wonderful manager I spoke about earlier in this chapter? She introduced me to an excellent tool that can assist with self-reflection: the Johari window.

Created by psychologists Joseph Luft and Harry Ingham, the exercise can be completed in work teams, or perhaps between you and a trusted colleague or mentor. It works like this:

1. From a list of adjectives, select those that you believe describe you – your personality and nature.
2. Ask your team members, colleagues or mentor to select, from the same list, the adjectives they believe describe you.
3. Sort the chosen adjectives into the grid pictured in figure 5.2:
   - Adjectives that both you and others selected go in the 'Open' or 'Arena' quadrant.
   - Adjectives that you did not select but that others did go in the 'Blind spot' quadrant.

- Adjectives that you selected but that others did not go in the 'Façade' quadrant.
- Adjectives that neither you nor others selected go in the 'Unknown' quadrant.

Figure 5.2: The Johari window

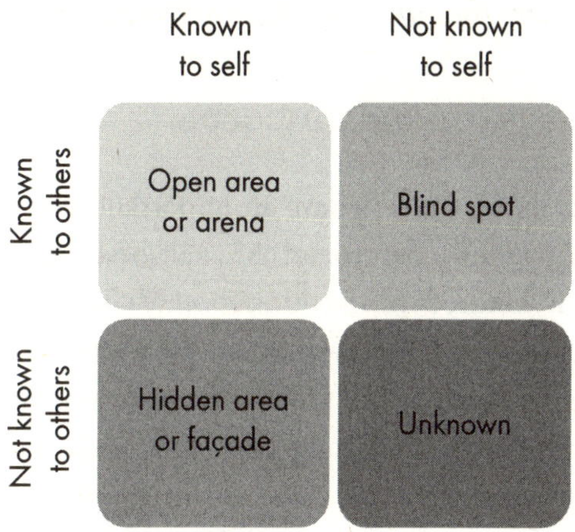

The most critical takeaway I gained from this tool is the importance of those adjectives that fall into the 'Blind spot' quadrant. These adjectives describe aspects of your personality or nature that others see, but that are unknown to you. To be able to see and open that hidden window is magical if you want to be the best you can be in your relationships with people and ultimately yourself. It's important to reflect on these adjectives and ponder why you don't see them in yourself when others do.

The 'Façade' quadrant is also fascinating, as these adjectives describe what you believe you project into the world but others don't see. Reflect on why this is the case. Why does your perception of yourself differ from what others know about you?

The Johari window is one that needs to be constantly opened and viewed. It's not a one-time event!

BE YOUR OWN BEST FRIEND

The most important conversations you'll ever have are the ones you'll have with yourself.

–

DAVID GOGGINS

It's a bit of a cliché, but I believe an important part of being self-aware is to be your own best friend. After all, best friends are not just great company, kindred spirits (think *Anne of Green Gables* – I loved those books!) and supportive – they are also there to be honest with you and stop you making the same mistakes again and again. I ask my best friends for feedback and advice, and I make it okay for them to be honest with me. When they tell me something that is hard to hear or unpleasant, I thank them. This encourages more of this open, trusted dialogue.

You can also do the same for yourself. You can be your own supporter, as well as giving yourself honest feedback. To do this, though, you need to have worked significantly on your self-awareness. You need to know yourself – and your triggers – intimately, as this is the only way you can really help yourself. Otherwise, it may be the blind leading the blind! These internal conversations can be very powerful in shaping who you are and the person you want to become.

I'm always using this self-best-friend tool myself. I talk to myself often, coaching myself in my head – even in meetings, where I find myself hilariously funny, almost a genius comic at times (I am honestly that funny!). However, I am also my harshest judge, and this is also something to be aware of. It's a matter of keeping it all in balance.

The benefit of being totally honest with yourself is that no-one else has to witness the truth, especially if you're not proud of your behaviour. Once you bring it to your conscious level, you are on the road to making positive changes. The next step is letting someone else acknowledge what you have accepted, without you reacting adversely. The shame about feedback, when it is critical or perceived as negative, is that you might recognise what is being said as accurate but react because your ego doesn't want to accept it. The next time this occurs, and you know the feedback to be true, agree and thank the person. You will witness instantaneously a change in the dynamics and demeanour of the conversation. Plus, you will be on the road to having that all-so-necessary respect.

***

If you are self-aware, you will always be employable. Employers actively seek out potential candidates who have high self-awareness. You will navigate the workplace landscape more easily, with awareness of the impact you have on other people. Best of all though, your heightened self-awareness will be better for you!

Reality check: how self-aware are you?

- If you could go back in time, what advice would you give yourself five years ago?
- In five years' time, if you are the same person, would you be okay with that?
- What puts an involuntary smile on your face?
- What was your last failure, mistake or disagreement? What did you learn from this?
- What are your trigger points?

- Who do you have as your trusted source of feedback? When was the last time they delivered you feedback that was a surprise or that you didn't want to hear? (If never, they are not the best source for honest feedback.)

TOP FIVE TAKEAWAYS

1. Consider feedback as a gift.
2. Look carefully for sensory feedback – it's likely to be the most honest form.
3. Find patterns and trends in the feedback you receive.
4. Make time for self-reflection. If it isn't a priority in your life, it won't happen.
5. Use the Johari window tool with your team or mentor, and reflect on what comes up for you.

6

Self-confidence

Each time we face our fear, we gain strength, courage, and confidence in the doing.

–

THEODORE ROOSEVELT

This quote had me at 'in the doing'. If you are not 'in the doing', you cannot build your self-confidence. And without self-confidence, your employability is shackled. For me, self-confidence is the most precious and treasured of all the attributes. It is the heart that ensures all the other attribute qualities have a beat, and in turn, the other attributes – when stretched and flexed – will strengthen self-confidence.

I know many talented people – friends, family, colleagues – who do not reach the realms of their dreams because their self-confidence is not strong enough to carry them there. And yet I know they have the capability to achieve what they dream of. It all comes down to self-confidence; when you have it, everything is easier, in work and life.

Without self-confidence, you will miss out on advancement and development opportunities – directly, because you won't put your hand up for them; and indirectly, because your boss won't have seen your capabilities. When you are confident, others will choose to put confidence in you.

In this chapter we will uncover the many ways in which self-confidence can improve your work and personal life. We'll look at:

- the relationship between self-confidence and self-esteem
- the 'confidence conundrum'
- how confidence affects you at work
- overconfidence
- how to build your self confidence.

SELF-CONFIDENCE AND SELF-ESTEEM

When thinking about self-confidence I always start with self-esteem. Self-esteem is a necessary ingredient for self-confidence. Self-confidence and self-esteem are often used interchangeably. They are both important behavioural concepts.

In simple terms, self-esteem is how you feel about yourself overall. According to Brian Tracy, author of *The Power of Self-Confidence*, 'the best definition of self-esteem is how much you like yourself.' Simple!

Self-confidence is having faith in your abilities. You can be self-confident in certain areas and have low self-esteem. Think of that person who is a gun IT expert at work, but then you meet for breakfast on the weekend and they can barely decide what to eat. Conversely, you can have healthy self-esteem and low confidence in a certain skill or ability. For me, that is true for cooking. I have faith, but my faith is that the roast dinner will not be good!

Psychologist Albert Bandura refers to belief in your ability as self-efficacy. His self-efficacy theory 'explains the relationship between the belief in one's abilities and how well a person actually performs the task.' If people have high self-efficacy in an area, they think, feel and behave in a way that contributes to and reinforces their success, and improves their personal satisfaction.

If you have high self-confidence and self-esteem, you are more likely to view obstacles as challenges to overcome. You recover from setbacks quickly, because you see failure not as a personal weakness but as a result of circumstances. In terms of employability, this is important because believing in your abilities affects your motivation and determination.

When you have self-confidence, other people want to be around you. Researchers have consistently found a link between confidence and success. Confident people are perceived as being more attractive. When you're self-confident, you believe you can handle challenges, which means you take more risks, which naturally leads to more opportunities.

When you are with people who possess healthy (or genuine) self-confidence, you may recognise that you feel 'safe' around them. They display a sense of confidence and appear in control, which rubs off on you. This feeling of safety is particularly important among business partners and in situations where you need to negotiate, make potentially difficult decisions or fix challenging problems.

Your self-esteem may vary depending on where you are at in your career and life. There are numerous theories as to why self-esteem peaks in middle age and then drops after retirement. According to research published by the American Psychological Association:

> *Midlife is a time of highly stable work, family and romantic relationships. People increasingly occupy positions of power and status, which might promote feelings of self-esteem. In contrast, older adults may be experiencing a change in roles such as an empty nest, retirement and obsolete work skills in addition to declining health.*

THE TRUTH ABOUT SELF-CONFIDENCE

Firstly, here is my truth: I struggled with writing this chapter the most out of all of them. I know how critical self-confidence is for employability, and how fragile it can be. How do you tell someone to be more self-confident when they lack self-confidence? This is often referred to as the 'confidence conundrum'. Mark Manson describes it well: 'In order to be happy or loved or successful, first you need to be confident... but to be confident, first you need to be happy or loved or successful.'

So, how do you break this cycle if you currently lack confidence? It's not simple, but it is achievable if you work at it.

The secret is that you need to be more comfortable in your own skin. Accept what you can change and what you cannot. If you want to change aspects of yourself, do it. The 'doing' will increase your levels of confidence and self-efficacy. Otherwise, whatever it is you feel you lack, learn to be okay with it. Brian Tracy says, 'In order to become self-confident, you need to work on building self-esteem and having self-acceptance.' The only way to be truly confident is to simply become comfortable with what you believe you lack. As Mark Manson says, 'confidence ... has nothing to do with being comfortable in what we achieve and everything to do with being comfortable in what we *don't* achieve.'

Think about a person who enters a social setting they don't appear to 'match'. At a simple level, let's say everyone is in a suit but they are wearing jeans and sneakers. They're not adhering to the social norms of the setting or group they have joined. And yet, they do not appear to be aware of it, or if they are, they're not concerned. This person has good self-esteem and is not attaching their worth to external factors such as appearance or expected superficial social norms. Or, think about a person who can hold their own in an intellectual discussion with a group of experts, even though they have no formal education. It is rare to meet these people, but when I do, I want to keep being around them.

We should never let our self-confidence or self-esteem depend on the behaviour of another person however much we may be humanly affected by him.

–

CARL JUNG

From the files

Several years ago I assisted with the selection of exchange students to go to Japan. The program was the typical one-year exchange for students in Year 11 or 12. The process is a panel interview for each student. On this day, one applicant stood out. In fact, she shone. She did everything wrong according to the 'textbook', but her self-confidence made it all okay.

She applied for the exchange program without her parents' knowledge, so she had no assistance or guidance. However, she walked into the interview, brimming with an excited smile. Her confidence was contagious.

Her application form was a disaster. It was riddled with mistakes, lines marked through and sections scribbled out. When we asked for clarity on one of the questions (because we could not read the answer clearly on her form), she looked puzzled, got up from her seat and asked to see the form. She gasped, showed humility, took responsibility with no attitude and said, 'Oh, I'm so sorry, I scanned you the wrong form. That was my practice form. This one here is the correct form. I have two copies.' She smiled. The 'real form' was great.

She did not let this hiccup derail her interview. In fact, she didn't bat an eye! She went back to smiles and her excited, enthused energy right away.

Her outfit was what no parent would advise to wear for such an important interview. Some students wore their school uniforms, others skirts or pants, ties and jackets. She chose to wear an outfit she made in sewing class, complete with patchwork squares in bright colours across her jumper. She happily and proudly told us she made her outfit, with zero thought that it might not be 'appropriate'. She felt good about herself, that was clear. And it was a joy to witness.

We asked her 'what if' questions and she answered them with ease, naturally, with very little nerves. She seemed to enjoy the challenge of the questions and was enthused to answer. She also happily shared funny stories of her family, pets and home life.

This girl was not afraid to be herself. She saw an opportunity and was not afraid to try. In fact, her enthusiasm and excitement were what propelled her forward, not her fear of failing. She was 'in the doing'.

She won that student exchange program hands down.

How confident are you?

Understanding where you sit with your levels of confidence will put you on the right track for employability. Reflect on the following questions, and be honest with yourself – nobody is listening!

- Are you comfortable saying 'no' to a request from a friend, family member or colleague?
- Are you comfortable disagreeing with someone's view if you don't believe it is right?
- Do you own your mistakes without blaming others?

- Do you take on responsibility, believing you are up to the task? Or do you quit before the end or not even take on a challenge in the first place, believing you will fail?
- Do you take on risks, go on the journey of trying, even with the possibility it may not turn out as expected or you might even fail?
- Are you plagued by negative self-talk?
- Do you become excited or fearful of new opportunities?

CONFIDENCE AT WORK

As you work on your self-confidence, you'll find your work life becoming easier. You won't be as caught up in your own self-doubt that detracts and distracts you at work. You will be more efficient, productive and focused. You will experience freedom from self-doubt and negative dialogue, and be happier to move out of your comfort zone. As you keep pushing yourself to try new things, you'll start to truly understand how failure and mistakes lead to growth. Your experience, knowledge and skill levels will increase. You will become more optimistic. Your relationships at work will be deeper. Interactions with your boss and team will improve.

You will communicate more effectively – confidence allows you to speak concisely and with clarity. It allows you to be your authentic self, communicating clearly and with no hidden agenda or passive-aggressive undertone. Most importantly and significantly your relaxed state will put others at ease, helping you forge deeper connections and relationships.

Having self-confidence does not mean you will not fail at some things, but it will assist you in coping with the setbacks. Your resilience will improve. You will always have your moments, because that's life, and without experiencing the other side you can't truly appreciate the great. You also can't be 100 per cent confident in all areas of your life, no matter who you are and what you have achieved. We all need the moments of self-doubt to continue and, on occasion, humble us – they become our areas to learn more about ourselves.

Having confidence means you will be more successful. An acceptance that failure is part of life will start to take root. Paradoxically, by being more willing to fail, you will actually succeed more, because you're not waiting for everything to be 100 per cent perfect before you act.

Michael Jordan is famous for, among other things, his ability to miss several shots in a row without registering even a flicker of concern, and then take the next without hesitation. Now *that's* confidence.

That's what employers want.

PEELING BACK THE LAYERS: OVERCONFIDENCE

We've all worked with someone who oozes self-confidence. They're extroverted, loud, assertive, a little 'in your face', charming and perhaps a tiny bit obnoxious.

During my career in recruitment, I've realised that a lot of the people who are perceived as extremely confident are actually not. It's a façade. Often, people who project confidence are actually masking their insecurities underneath. In this case, confidence sends a strong message to stay away and not question the person too closely – if you did, you might realise how much the person is actually afraid and unsure of their worth and abilities.

When you meet this type of person, a part of you may have been impressed by them or their demeanour, but at the same time your intuition may have been telling you something was amiss. You might have concluded that you simply did not quite gel with them, but as we discussed in chapter 4, it's likely you were picking up on their subtle, nonverbal cues. Subconsciously, you were aware of some mismatching, misalignment, inconsistency, and incongruence. These are all signs of the person's inner lack of confidence.

This situation is different to when you fake confidence in certain situations, like job interviews, as a way of putting your best self forward. Constant overconfident behaviour is bravado to stop others questioning and getting too close to you, and therefore seeing what you believe you may be 'lacking'.

If you believe you might fall into this trap, it's important to be aware of this and reflect on it. Continual overconfident bravado limits your employability. By not allowing people to assist you, your working relationships will be impacted and likely exist only at a superficial level. Your learning and development will also be stunted.

Remember: when you hide parts of yourself, you come across as fake, and this diminishes your ability to connect with others. You can't connect deeply with those you mistrust.

HOW TO BUILD YOUR SELF-CONFIDENCE

So, how can you learn to be comfortable in your own skin and at peace with whatever it is you 'lack'? It's not as simple as 'go for a run', although that has its place! Here's what I've learned.

1. **Be aware of your self-talk:** coach yourself every time your thoughts wander into harmful territory. If they go to a negative place, especially to do with yourself or your image, literally say 'Stop!' even out loud! Or say to yourself, 'I'll think about this tomorrow.' It takes some practice, but it works. Brian Tracy refers to the law of concentration, saying that whatever you dwell on continually grows in your reality. This is a similar concept to Martin Seligman's learned optimism theory, which in essence talks of how positive or good outcomes happen to optimistic people. Seligman explains how optimists expect a positive outcome, so their behaviours, actions and communications all manifest in that manner. They are more likely to have assistance in achieving their goals as they talk to people about what they are doing, in a dialogue of enthusiasm

and excitement. We talk more about this in chapter 7. Dwell on positive self-talk, not the negative.

2. **Congratulate yourself:** celebrate your achievements. Even if you believe you haven't achieved anything, you'll find you have if you start to make a list! Each day think of something good you have done – even if it's the same thing – until you free your mind to see other achievements.
3. **Be grateful:** it works. Daily, as soon as you wake up, think of five things you are grateful for. It will shift your outlook, only a little, but that incremental change will play out significantly in other parts of your life. Watch how quickly you reel off the list after just a week – and it grows. Gratitude takes you away from viewing the negative or bad in your life and brings you to what you do have and can be appreciative of.
4. **Know what your 'thing' is:** what are you good at? We all have something. What is it that comes easy to you at work? Find it and repeat it to yourself!
5. **Take pride in your appearance:** this is not about vanity; it's about self-love and self-worth. When you feel good about how you are presenting yourself to the world, it changes how you interact, relate, react and be. It can alter your outlook for the day. This is even more applicable with working from home becoming more prevalent. It's a novelty to be in your tracksuit pants on occasion, but it can be a slippery slope. You may be surprised in what you can achieve when working from home and maintaining pride in your appearance – even if no-one sees you that day, you will see yourself!
6. **Act positively:** even if you are not feeling it. This will help your self-confidence as people will view you a certain way, you will then react positively back, and it goes on. Also smile – it works!
7. **Be kind and give:** this is my go-to, no matter how I am feeling.

8. **Be well-prepared for work meetings:** know what is on the agenda, who is attending and what is required of you. Knowing who the participants are and what their role is will give you the confidence to build meaningful dialogue. Ensure you read any briefing papers beforehand and consider your responses. You will be more likely to contribute to the meeting and understand the nuances of the discussion.
9. **Be organised at home:** it helps to feel in control, even if it's just little things.
10. **Know what is important to you:** and learn how to say no to anything that doesn't meet that criteria.
11. **Don't give up or quit**: even if it means investing in time after work, watch the difference in your performance and engagement and see your confidence increase.
12. **Tick small things off your list:** don't procrastinate.
13. **At work, if an issue or mistake occurs, do not melt:** focus on the solution. Rather than blaming or complaining, move to action straight away.
14. **Exercise:** this is my personal number one. Exercising every day helps me cope with pressure and deal with whatever is coming my way that day. Even if it's just a walk, you will feel better. And while you are doing it, smile at everyone you see!
15. **Set goals:** according to Tracy, 'there are no unrealistic goals, only unrealistic timelines.' Setting goals requires self-confidence and simultaneously builds self-confidence. When you have the courage to write down what you really want, you'll find your self-esteem and self-confidence both improve, and you'll feel more powerful. Tracy suggests writing down your major goals each day in the present tense – 'I achieve' or 'I am', without referring to what you wrote yesterday.

***

When you work on your self-confidence, your belief in your own skills and abilities will increase and you will grow into who you really are as person. Working on your self-confidence will help you accept yourself and feel happy about the person you are. We all want to work with people who are confident. Having confidence is good for you and for those around you.

Before you diagnose yourself with depression or low self-esteem, make sure that you are not surrounded by fools.

–

SIGMUND FREUD

Reality check: how self-confident are you?

- When was the last time you tried something totally new?
- When did you last ask for help at work?
- When did you last offer to assist someone at work?
- When was the last time you spoke up at a meeting to contribute a new idea?
- When was the last time you said something negative/positive to yourself?

TOP FIVE TAKEAWAYS

1. If you have high self-confidence and self-esteem, you are more likely to view obstacles as challenges to overcome.
2. Self-confidence impacts all your other attributes.
3. To build self-confidence, you need to be more comfortable in your own skin. Accept what you can change about yourself and what you cannot.
4. Having confidence means you will be more successful at work and in life.
5. We all want to work with people who are confident. Having confidence is good for you and for those around you.

7

Optimism

My barn having burned down,
I can now see the moon.

–

MIZUTA MASAHIDE

Optimism is your powerhouse attribute. It is the booster for all your other attributes. It causes you to think differently and feel differently. Buddha said, 'The mind is everything. What you think, you become.' Your thoughts, consciously or unconsciously, drive your actions and behaviour.

Optimistic people are far more likely to discover new ways of working and run after new ideas and opportunities. They believe they can achieve whatever they set their mind to, so they are happy to try new things, explore new ideas and listen to other people. For optimists, the thought of failing rarely arises – the excitement of achieving their dreams is what keeps them going. If you are an optimist, you put in the effort because you believe there will be a good outcome.

Every manager wants optimists on their team. Optimistic people are generally happy, have high energy levels and bring creativity, inspiration and a hopeful approach to the workplace.

In this chapter we will uncover the myriad of ways in which optimism can improve your employability and happiness. We'll look at:

- the link between optimism and employability
- why optimism is good for you
- the Pollyanna Principle
- how to avoid contagious negativity.

OPTIMISM AND EMPLOYABILITY

Optimism is critical for motivation and performance and is essential for achieving goals. It has been linked to an intrinsic motivation to work harder, endure stressful circumstances and display goal-focused behaviour. No wonder recruiters and hiring managers love it when they can detect optimism in candidates during the interview process! In fact, research from the Foundation for Young Australians found that an optimistic mindset can speed up candidates' job hunt by two months.

Optimism breeds optimism. If you have an optimistic outlook, you'll be the one your managers and colleagues most enjoy working with – especially during challenging times. My go-to person at work will always be the person who is highly optimistic. Under pressure, positive people are solutions-focused – unlike pessimists, who tend to require cajoling during difficult times.

It should come as no surprise that there is a strong link between entrepreneurship and optimism. Research shows that entrepreneurs are usually high in dispositional optimism. Optimism is also a necessary element for innovation – it drives curiosity, which fosters invention.

OPTIMISM IS GOOD FOR YOU – IT'S A FACT

Firstly, and most importantly, optimism is good for you! Many studies have shown that optimistic people are happier and healthier. Having an optimistic approach to life is key to attaining happiness. Even our life expectancy improves. According to Harvard Medical School, research tells us that an optimistic outlook early in life can predict better health and even a lower rate of death. It's not only high levels of optimism that have a positive effect. Even slightly erring on the optimistic side rather than having a pessimistic view can have a startling effect. Interestingly, it's low levels of pessimism, rather than high levels of optimism, that are associated with better health. Pessimists expect that negative outcomes are more likely to occur than positive outcomes. Pessimism is associated with anxiety, depression, sleep disorders, hostility, high blood pressure and heart disease.

Optimism is very much a state of mind and a choice you make in where you want your attention to focus. Your thoughts and beliefs are a powerful playground, and they have a strong influence on the way you see the world and your circumstances.

THE POLLYANNA PRINCIPLE

Did you read the book *Pollyanna* when you were a child? (I did!) The book portrays a cheerful and optimistic girl who always looks on the bright side and has a huge positive impact on those around her. The Pollyanna Principle refers to the tendency to remember pleasant and positive memories and recall neutral events as more positive than they really were. Many highly intelligent, analytic people dismiss and resist the importance of optimism and commonly refer to optimists as being 'Pollyannas' – the idea being that optimists are excessively cheerful, with the emphasis on the word 'excessive'. The underlying meaning is that Pollyannas lack real-world experience and don't consider risks or reality.

Considering reality and weighing up risks are necessary behaviours required in viewing a situation for what it is – seeing the situation in as truthful a light as possible. However, this does not take away the necessary ability to see the upside and seek out opportunities – the 'where to from here' thinking. Having your eyes wide open so you can see it all – the good and the bad – is a must, not just in analysing a problem but for life skills in general. However, the way you view the 'bad' is important. According to Martin Seligman, who we met in chapter 6, 'The genius of evolution lies in the dynamic tension between optimism and pessimism continually correcting each other.'

Excessive cheerfulness is not the type of optimism that is likely to increase your employability. Have you ever expressed frustration or annoyance at work (which, by the way, is entirely normal), only to be shut down by an overly and irritatingly optimistic person? This is where optimism is hijacked by naivety and possibly poor emotional intelligence (EQ).

Optimists and pessimists don't necessarily stand on the opposite side of the pendulum, since we all have traits of both qualities. Optimism is how you see the world, but with sensibility and pragmatism. Pragmatism is about taking a realistic and sensible approach to life, and making peace with the fact that things may either go south or north. Pragmatists will do their risk analysis and contingency plans before starting anything. They prepare themselves for both the best and the worst. Pragmatic optimism is faith and belief, but not blind hope.

From the files

Many years ago I was asked to deliver a talk to senior call centre managers. I was nervous. My manager encouraged me by saying it would be good for me – it would boost my profile and there are all sorts of positives that exposure like this may bring. I knew it would be good for my professional development, but I was scared. I had never enjoyed public speaking. Even speaking up in management meetings was a challenge for me. Up until this point, I had avoided all opportunities of public speaking that came my way, but this time I bit the bullet and said yes.

Not only did I prepare well, I made sure to feel good on the day. I bought a new suit and went to gym super early. I caught a taxi to the gym, so I could be 100 per cent on time with no unexpected delays. I finished my workout and felt great! Had a shower, did my make-up and started to get dressed. Underwear, shirt, stockings, jacket – tick, tick, tick, tick. But wait ... where's my skirt? No skirt! I searched my gym bag to no avail. I called my husband and he finally located my skirt, strung out on the bushes on the roundabout on our street, right where I jumped into the taxi.

I had 40 minutes until my talk. There wasn't enough time for my husband to bring my skirt to me. The shops were not open. Maybe I could cancel? I considered it for a moment (I mean, it was a legitimate excuse, was it not?) but I realised I had no choice. I had to go through with it for the sake of my career, and my own self-worth.

I delivered that talk with my bottom half clad in gym clothing and my top half in corporate attire. I decided I could use my odd appearance as a way to break the ice and capture people's attention from the beginning.

It was a silver lining.

Although my imperfection on the day was not deliberate, later on I learned that my optimism and desire to make the best of the situation had directed me towards the Pratfall Effect. First studied by social psychologist Elliot Aronson in 1966, the Pratfall Effect is where someone who is considered highly competent is found to be more likeable when they perform an everyday blunder. This is thought to be because competent people are sometimes viewed by others as superhuman, so a small mistake makes them seem more human and likeable.

My optimism (and courage) saved me that day. Had I been pessimistic and cancelled the presentation, the consequences for both my reputation at work, my manager's belief in me and my own self-belief and self-confidence could have been dire. In the end, I pulled off the presentation and the whole experience made me so much more confident in my own ability to make the best of every challenge.

NEGATIVITY IS CONTAGIOUS

Are you that person that bad things always happen to? The bird poops on your fresh blow-dry just before an important meeting; you always seem to get stuck in bad traffic; you catch the bus that breaks down; you always lose your umbrella; your plane is always delayed. And then, do you come in to work and dump a diatribe on your colleagues, blaming all of these events on 'bad luck'?

Do you tend to complain a lot? Do you shy away from trying new things – even a different route to work or a new coffee shop? Do you worry a lot? If so, there might be some lessons to be learned for you.

Here is a manager's secret: we know negativity is bad for team morale and productivity. It spreads just like a virus and can wipe out whole teams. All it takes is one person with a pessimistic attitude to bring down an entire team. Studies show that employee engagement decreases significantly through emotional exhaustion when negativity is rife in the workplace.

I am not referring to people who air the odd complaint – that is healthy and normal. I'm referring to negativity that has set in and is habitual. Like all habits, it increases its intensity if it's allowed to fester. It becomes second nature.

From the files

Several years ago I travelled to the UK for work and my friend, an ex-colleague who was now managing director of a recruitment company, offered me the use of their office space for my short time in London. 'Great!' I thought, 'I can focus and get through some work.'

On the first day, I joined the team's work in progress (WIP) meeting, just to be a part of it and see what I could learn. As is typical with morning meetings in recruitment, the idea is to set the tone for the day – which should be positive. The meeting included an announcement of a team member's promotion, and everyone left the meeting with goals, focus and a buoyant feeling.

During the day, while my friend was in meetings, I tried to get through my ever-increasing pile of work. Instead, I found myself observing the manoeuvres and machinations of a staff member called Andrew – a very experienced 'Negatar' (the name I have coined for negativity in human form).

Not long after the meeting, his first comment was, 'We won't reach that target – the budgets are never achievable.' As the day progressed, I saw him go from group to group, desk to desk and express similar opinions.

During the day, a junior consultant made a placement and was expressing her excitement. Instead of joining in on the excitement, Andrew gave his 'advice': 'Do you have the contract? If not, don't count your chickens. I know your candidate has accepted, but perhaps ask them if they would like extra time to consider the offer?' Not only was Andrew negative, but in the guise of providing advice, he was trying to thwart the junior consultant and the business's success. He had also deflated the consultant's achievement, making her feel uncertain.

Because I was only an observer in the team, I was able to see the situation without any bias attached, and I could see how Andrew's behaviour was affecting morale and productivity.

Constant negativity can be a huge drain on a team's energy. From an employability perspective, it's important to keep a check on the negativity you bring to work. Take a moment to consider the effect your attitude might be having on your workmates.

It's important to be aware of the effect negativity and pessimism can have on your employability. It affects your interpersonal skills in so many ways, and managers can spot it a mile away (another manager's secret!). If your pessimism is at the stage of being habitual, you will be shrouded by it. It will affect your body language, tone and even the way you move. Negativity is like a dark cloud, pervading your thoughts, behaviour and actions. Like oversized luggage, it will weigh you down.

A final point on negativity: some people wear their pessimism as a badge of honour, claiming 'It's just who I am.' If this is you, you might want to consider where your negativity or pessimism is coming from. Use your self-awareness to dig deep and uncover your triggers. It could be a temporary phase or more long-term. Either way, if you recognise it, you are on the way to helping yourself. Use your own best friend to assist with the analysis and self-talk.

***

An optimistic outlook keeps you on an even keel at work and helps you achieve more. It will increase your self-efficacy and confidence as well as your resilience. Optimistic people deal with stress more easily than others; they do not overcomplicate the situation and make plans to move forward. People operating in this way are not only highly employable, but also well respected, likeable and highly sought after as team members.

Reality check: how optimistic are you?

- Have you ever been annoyed by someone's cheerfulness?
- When faced with a setback, do you let yourself be waylaid or look for a solution?
- What was the most recent setback you experienced, and what was the silver lining from it?
- Have you witnessed negativity in the office? How did it make you feel?
- When was the last time you came up with a good solution or idea at work?

TOP FIVE TAKEAWAYS

1. If you have an optimistic outlook, you'll be the one your managers and colleagues most enjoy working with.
2. Optimism is good for your happiness and health.
3. Pragmatic optimism is faith and belief, but not blind hope.
4. Negativity is bad for team morale and productivity.
5. Consider where your negativity or pessimism is coming from.

PART II

Milestones and life

The moon is the first milestone on the road to the stars.

–

ARTHUR C. CLARKE

CAREERS DON'T STAND STILL, and neither does life. As you progress from the beginning of your career to midcareer to retirement (or not!), you will pass through a range of different milestones that can have a significant impact on your employability. Sometimes it might feel like life is getting in the way of your career, but there are actions you can take at each stage of life to stay employable, even when your focus is on some other aspect of your life.

During my career I've recruited and mentored people across every career stage. In my observations, there are four main stages you may progress through on your career journey. These include:

1. **Exploration and establishment:** in this stage you're figuring out career options and moving from education to work: finding a job, learning the basics of it and where you fit, all while learning the different facets of the business world and the people in it. In this stage you can feel like there are limitless opportunities – which can be exciting and, at the same time, daunting.

2. **Advancement:** in this stage you are progressing along a career path, reaching goals, becoming more of an expert, and either going on to greater heights or perhaps levelling off. Your horizons are opening. You may start caring more about whether your career carries prestige, reputation or financial gains, and where you stand in your chosen industry or society.

3. **Maintenance:** this stage is when you're maintaining productivity while no longer learning about the job. You may have mastered your skills and perhaps you are mentoring someone, or evaluating your career goals. At this stage you may care more about the meaning derived from your career.

Generally, you know who you are and where you are going. You may be more involved in social causes and philanthropic work, or nurturing your hobbies and interests outside of work.

4. **Retirement:** in this stage you may be phasing out of the workforce having fulfilled your legacy. You might be considering how to spend your 'retirement' years. Paradoxically, this stage is comparable to your starting point, except for the years of experience! It is a transition phase and can be a little scary for some, but if you have something significant to look forward to, you will find excitement and hope to keep you engaged and provide meaning. You see new opportunities and priorities and typically, this is when you are more focused on yourself.

Of course, you may not follow a straight pathway from stage one to four. You might meander between the stages, change careers, have a career break or start again in a different industry. The days of spending most of your working life at one organisation have gone. The shifting sands of your career journey will take you to many different territories, including an occasional landing in 'no-man's land'. Your employability will ensure you see this through. As you progress through the different stages, your values, needs and beliefs will change, together with your life's conditions – and your employability will require focus and appropriate engagement at each stage.

It's possible that one chapter in this part of the book will speak more directly to your current situation. Still, it's worthwhile perusing through the other chapters for valuable information that doesn't fit neatly into a single set of circumstances. As the world changes rapidly and you experience unexpected events, your job or desire and ambition that seemed constant and stable yesterday can be different tomorrow. Be open and well equipped to respond to career opportunities as well as career 'shocks'. These career shocks can hugely impact the stage's predictability and introduce new trends that you are yet to understand and experience.

8

Graduates and school leavers

Remembering that you are going to die
is the best way I know to avoid the trap of thinking
you have something to lose. You are already naked.
There is no reason not to follow your heart.

-

STEVE JOBS

It's so exciting being a new graduate, whether you've just finished school or university. You're at the exploration and establishment stage, moving from education to work: feeling adventurous, figuring out career options, finding a job, learning the basics of it and working out where you fit. You are likely to be full of dreams and may feel pressure in choosing your first job. You're probably already looking for a job that has a higher meaning – one that is aligned to what you perceive as your calling.

If this is you, you can relax. This phase is not necessarily about finding an 'ideal job', but the *right* job to take you on the long journey of discovery: exploring, acquiring knowledge, practising, developing, and learning about others as you learn about yourself.

Hopefully, you are also hungry to show what you are made of – to share the unique gifts you possess, making a difference to your future employer, or possibly to the whole world. You may be intensely keen and in a hurry to make a difference. While it is admirable to see that passion, remember that this phase of your career is when you build your skills and confidence and gain credibility. This takes time. The more credibility you earn, the more you will be taken seriously, and the further your voice will travel. Patience might not always be a 'friend' of youth and passion, but if you are to succeed during this phase of your career maturation, you will need to master it as best as you can. If prudence is the mother of all virtues, then patience is the father.

Reading this chapter, you may also be a parent or friend of a graduate or school leaver. I hope you concur with the advice given here, as it is tough love in some instances!

This chapter is packed full of insights and advice for those about to begin their careers. We'll look at:

- job readiness
- the importance of your personal brand
- exploring career options
- work experience and interning
- digging deep when competition is tough
- top tips for your first job.

JOB READINESS

In this first phase of your career, employability means being job ready.

If you are reading this chapter as a graduate or school leaver, you are ahead of the pack. Picking up this book means you are already grasping the importance of being employable early on.

Over the past 20 years, the share of the Australian population that holds a degree at a bachelor level or above has more than tripled, reaching 28.2 per cent in 2019. However, according to research by Pure Profile and career strategy firm TwoPointZero, one in three young university graduates do not find work in their chosen field. This may seem alarming, but it just means you need to take your employability seriously even before you've found your first position. You need to be job ready.

You might be wondering, what does being job ready actually mean? Essentially, it means possessing the crucial skills and knowledge that will help you land your first job after graduation and kick-start a great career. According to the Hon. Dan Tehan, former federal Minister for Education, 'It is essential that students are exposed to how contemporary workplaces operate so they can hit the ground running from day one of the job.' Universities Australia suggests activities such as formal work placements, projects with industry or community groups, fieldwork and practical simulations could help prepare you to hit the ground running when you start your first job.

My advice is to embrace every practical experience you can throughout your study – including part-time work. This will provide you with skills in preparation for your first 'career job', and make your application more attractive to employers. The classroom gives you the theory while work experience, particularly if it's in a related industry, gives you practical experience. You will also perceive your future job more realistically. How many people thought they wanted to be a nurse or doctor to 'help people', only to be confronted with the reality of what the job really entails? I was in this category, until I did my work experience in a hospital!

To be job ready you must always be thinking of your competitive advantage. Having a competitive advantage over other job seekers is a major part of being employable. What activities or work experiences can you get involved in at university that will give you an advantage over your peers?

Research from the Foundation for Young Australians found four significant factors that can help you secure your first full-time job more quickly. These include:

- **Study that teaches enterprise skills like problem-solving, teamwork and communication:** this can speed up your transition to full-time work by 17 months.
- **Relevant paid work experience:** this can speed up your transition by up to 12 months.
- **Pursuing a career that has strong future growth prospects:** this can speed up your transition by five months.
- **An optimistic mindset:** this can speed up your transition by two months.

While work experience that is relevant to your future industry is ideal, any type of casual job – such as in hospitality or retail – will be very well regarded. These jobs before graduation are your training wheels, so expect to make mistakes – it is par for the course. They will help you develop the 'soft skills' employers value, particularly communication skills, which you'll build while dealing with customers, peers and managers. This kind of experience will give you confidence, competence and self-assurance. Most of this you won't even realise you are acquiring, and it will further strengthen your competitive advantage.

Longevity and tenure are always well regarded when it comes to casual jobs. If you have held four part-time jobs at six months each, this won't come across as strongly as having one part-time job for two years. If you jump around between employers too often, the perception could be that you struggled to commit or hold down a job – that there may have been a problem with your attendance, the quality of your work, your attitude or your strength under pressure.

Excellent marks at school or university are great, but will only get you so far. Have those marks in conjunction with extracurricular interests and some form of paid employment while studying, and you will streak ahead.

YOUR PERSONAL BRAND AND REPUTATION

Word of mouth is extremely important when it comes to employability, and you can start developing your reputation long before beginning your first career role.

When you apply for graduate roles, you'll be expected to supply references – these are people who are willing to vouch for you and speak to your prospective new employer about your skills and attributes. Working while you're studying is an excellent way to connect with professional referees.

As you conduct yourself in your casual job, think of how you want to be perceived by your employer. Do you want to be known for reliability and trustworthiness? Then be reliable and punctual. Ask for responsibilities and honour them. This will mean that when it comes time to ask your managers to be your referees, they will only be too willing to assist.

There is only one thing worse than not having credible people (references) vouching for you, and that is having noncredible people as your referees. Your relatives or best mate won't cut it! Teachers or university tutors are passable, but not as convincing as an independent, professional referee.

References are particularly important for new graduates, for two reasons:

1. Since you don't have a lot of experience, it can be difficult for the interviewer to assess your skills and competencies from an interview.
2. Many new graduates have had limited experience with interviews, so may be nervous. Your references will bring you to life.

In addition to the references you provide, you may also be subject to off-the-record references. These are another manager's secret, and they happen all the time. It's a small world in many industries and communities, and your future employer may know someone who has worked or studied with you before. Often the views of these people are not based on your actual work output but the perception of your reliability and interpersonal skills. Do not underestimate the opinions of people you know who may provide these off-the-record references. While you can't control other people's perceptions, you can manage your behaviour.

Your future employers will also seek to verify your reputation via an 'evidence reference' – that is, checking out your presence online. Ensure that your public image is appropriate and aligned with your reputation and how you want to be seen by others. How you communicate via social platforms, and what style of language you are using, is also critical. Even incorrect spelling could be an alarm bell. Your future employer will not excuse bad behaviour just because you posted at 2 am from the back seat of an Uber.

At the same time, your positive presence on professional platforms, such as LinkedIn, is highly regarded. Ensure your profile looks professional and that you have started to develop your network.

If your actions (what is visible to others) align with your intentions (thoughts that are not visible to others), you have nothing to worry about!

CAREER DREAMING

This is a really fun time for career exploration. Open your mind to what you would love to do and be. Dream. Be open to opportunities and take them up. Tick off as many new experiences as you can – they are a great way to expose yourself to different ideas and learn more about what makes your heart sing. Be curious and explorative.

You might surprise yourself by falling in love with a field you hadn't considered before, or discovering that the job that seemed so attractive in the beginning may not be the right fit for you.

Here are some ideas for experiences you might like to get involved with while you're at school or university:

- Take on extra responsibilities in your casual job.
- Do a short course.
- Attend a conference.
- Join a planning committee in your local community.
- Volunteer for an event or cause.
- Join a sports team.
- Join a club or society at university (or, better still, apply for a leadership position in your club of choice).
- Volunteer for your university's Open Day.
- Join a mentoring program.
- Go overseas on exchange.

By putting yourself out there, you'll be seen and noticed. Don't wait in the background, expecting to be discovered by chance.

Make time to dream about your future career and where you see yourself. What is it you are aspiring to do or be in the future? Who is it that inspires you? Do your research. If there's a particular workplace or job role you're interested in, look up employees at that company or in that field on LinkedIn. Check out their career and employment history and look for any trends. You may be surprised to see where they started out. Everyone starts somewhere – it is what you do with the choices and opportunities you have access to that determines the path to your dream job. Remember, your first job won't necessarily be your dream job, and that's okay (see figure 8.1).

Figure 8.1: The road to your dream job

From the files

A client of mine, a human resources director at a media company, presents at universities each year as part of her search for talented graduates. Before her presentation, she contacts the cohort of students and tells them about the great intern opportunities she has available. Each year, the cohort comprises between 380 and 450 students. All students are invited to the presentation, but only around 150 to 200 attend. After the presentation, my client invites the students to submit their résumés. On average, around 50 do so. From the 50, she then contacts 20 students to invite for an interview. Only 10 are keen. Four do not show. She is left with six to choose from. That is six candidates from circa 380 to 450 students. Can you see your opportunity now?

Another of my clients is HR Director of a global organisation that employs more than 50,000 people – a big player. He presents each year at a university, across the disciplines of law, economics, engineering and marketing. The attendance numbers when he presents are under 200.

I am confident these stats and figures are not isolated. If I think back to my own experience at university of applying for the exchange program to Japan, I am confident the numbers who applied to that were also low – probably because they, too, wanted to spend their summer at the beach rather than in a foreign country! You may have to sacrifice something fun to get a golden career opportunity, but it's worth it, and the numbers suggest you have a pretty good chance of getting what you go for.

Make the most of every opportunity presented. Even better, create opportunities for yourself.

WORK EXPERIENCE AND INTERNING

We have established that work experience and interning are essential! Securing these appointments and working them in with your other responsibilities can be a challenge, but it's well worth it. In this section, we'll explore how to get an internship position and how to make the most of it.

Make your application stand out

Here are my tips to help you secure your place in the internship program:

1. Remember, it is a numbers game! You will have to apply and keep applying, but do not apply randomly. Tailor each application and follow up.
2. Create a list of inspiring companies and approach them – do not wait for opportunities to come to you. Put yourself out there. Everyone loves courageous individuals.
3. If you don't hear back, follow up.

4. Don't be afraid to approach high-ranking employees when you're asking for an internship placement. Just be courteous and respectful of their time.
5. If you have a casual job, consider seeking out an intern role within that company. For example, if you work in retail and studying marketing, you could approach the head office for an internship.
6. If you're studying at university, check if your campus careers service has any programs or opportunities you can take advantage of.

It's all about attitude

When you are interning, to be frank, your attitude is your biggest currency. If you have limited skills or experience, your attitude is what will impress.

Whether it's paid or unpaid it's important to treat the intern role like a proper job. Don't think of it as a box you need to tick off as part of your degree. This will be plainly clear to your employer (remember how we spoke about body language and tone in chapter 4?).

Be proactive and show initiative and enthusiasm. It can be as simple as unloading the dishwasher in the office kitchen, restocking the printer or tidying the reception area. This kind of contribution reflects your attitude, work ethic and engagement. If you are not busy, make yourself busy.

It goes without saying that you must be on time, every time. Do not call in sick (unless you genuinely need to), and dress appropriately for an office environment – neat, tidy and clean.

Seeking feedback

In this early stage of your career, you need as much guidance as possible. Someone who will be honest with you, and point out the areas where you already show great potential as well as those that might need improvement, is an asset. Don't be afraid to ask your manager for feedback; it will assist you immensely once you start searching for your permanent role. Getting used to accepting others' opinions and evaluation early on will create a good habit for you. See it as a tool to help you grow.

Through this feedback, you may find out you are talented in areas that you never considered before. You may suddenly start looking at jobs and industries that you were less interested in previously, perhaps because you feared you didn't possess the right criteria for success. Your own opinions about your abilities and skills are essential, but they are also subjective.

Your whole life, you will be receiving feedback about your performance and you will be providing feedback for others. Learning the art of how to receive invaluable insights about your working style and habits will improve your communication, self-confidence, the ability to take on challenging conversations without becoming paralysed, and much more.

Crave honest feedback from others because they want you to succeed!

Once you transition to the next stage of your career and life, you will look at your internships and work experience roles with gratitude. I can promise you that.

DIGGING DEEP

Some graduate opportunities are incredibly competitive and applying for them requires a whole new level of persistence, hard work and bravery.

The wife of a great friend of mine has always been incredibly smart, bright and successful. People always thought she was blessed or that what she had achieved had 'come easily'. It never occurred to them how hard she worked for what she achieved. At dinner one night, she told me about an additional master's degree she had applied for – at one of *the* universities in the US. They only allowed a handful of applicants in each year and, because of the industry, a higher proportion of positions were offered to men. The odds were stacked against her. She had applied for a spot the year before and had not made it through the difficult application process. The interview was the clincher: it was a three-hour-long competency-based panel interview and was gruelling. My friend was not good in these situations. Tests and research she was comfortable with, but being an introvert, interviews were not her forte. Unfortunately, she didn't get onto the course the first time round.

However, she didn't give up. Second time round, her solution was to prepare better for the interview component of the application. And she did so, for a year. She researched every conceivable style of question that could be asked and compiled her answers. She practised saying them, becoming acutely familiar with them, making it impossible not to recall each one. She went into the panel interview the following year a changed person – self-assured, confident, and able to articulate what was always there. And she nailed it!

The journey of applying herself in this manner brought about so many additional learnings, growth and development, which is the point of the story. Pursuing opportunities is not always about the opportunity itself – it is what you gain along the way that can guide you to other pathways.

YOUR FIRST CAREER ROLE

Your first job is something you will hopefully always look back on with fondness. It's a stepping stone to your dream career and will set the tone for the rest of your working life. It's an exciting time, but it can also be very challenging! Let's take a look at some techniques and tips for making your first job a smooth ride and getting the most you can out of the experience.

The job hunt

Job searching can be laborious, challenging and even disempowering at times, particularly when you're looking for a graduate role, which can be highly competitive. Here are my tips for finding the right job for you:

- Check online job boards like SEEK and LinkedIn regularly and set up alerts.
- Manage your expectations. You may feel your skills and experience place you 'above' entry-level roles, but if a role provides a stepping stone into your chosen industry and the opportunity to grow and develop, do consider it. Know that most graduates don't land their dream graduate role straight up.
- Keep your LinkedIn profile up-to-date and make sure you are listed as 'open to opportunities'. Use LinkedIn to connect with people in your industry and follow your dream workplaces.
- Create a list of organisations you would like to work for and research their websites. See if they offer graduate programs or junior roles.
- Focus on the opportunity, not on the salary. There is plenty of time to grow your earnings as you progress in your career.
- Make the most of any career fairs, presentations or networking events that your school or university is holding.
- Consider volunteering for a charitable organisation or doing extra shifts at your casual job while you search for your full-time role. This is a great way to keep yourself motivated and facilitate skill and network building.
- Research and sign up for industry e-newsletters that include job opportunities.
- Reach out to a recruiter. Recruitment agencies can assist in 'selling' you to companies. Look for junior roles advertised with

recruitment companies that are in the industry that is appealing to you. In approaching recruiters, I would suggest a phone call – and have your résumé ready to send, demonstrating your on-point tech skills!

The early days in your new job

Once you land a job, celebrate! Embrace the opportunity and have gratitude. Gratitude is more than just feeling appreciation for the good things you have in your life. It also helps you connect to something larger than yourself.

Your first priority when you begin your new role is to meet the team and figure out who's who. You should find out who does what in your team and division – their roles, titles and tenure. You should also know who the CEO is and what they look like. If you happen to run into them in the lift, you will kick yourself if you don't know!

If you haven't already done so as part of your interview preparation, find out who your company's competitors are.

Understand your job description – what is required of you and the expectations that come with it. You want to know what we refer to at EST10 as 'the invisible ink' – the requirements of your job that are unwritten. It's those underlying, invisible 'small dots' that are needed to connect the whole picture. Often job descriptions are quite generic, especially if they are written to fit into a specific salary band or organisational template. Use your time with your manager to probe your role and ask about the expectations that may not be covered in the job description. Always know what is expected of you, especially in terms of deadlines and deliverables. If you do not understand what to do, ask.

Be a culture detective so you can work out the cultural norms quickly. These can include things like the dress code and expectations around breaks, phone etiquette and communication style. Observe and ask questions. Asking questions is a positive trait and providing there are good boundaries, sharing experiences, insights, and information helps to build relationships and the bonds that go with it. Life, whether professional or personal, is all about relationships.

Entitlement and manners

You might feel that you deserve a job and that you are quite talented in certain areas, however you are not *entitled* to a job.

If you have a degree, it may give you an advantage, but it is not an automatic ticket to employment. Your degree may show your employer that you have intellectual abilities and the discipline to finish your studies, but that's it. As harsh as this sounds, you are entering the workforce on the bottom rung, and while you have plenty to contribute, you won't impress anyone if you purport to know it all.

Manners will get you far. You might consider me old-fashioned, but think about the age of the people who have employed you – your manager, or your manager's manager. To be employable you must consider what might be important to your employer, and I can guarantee that courtesy is high on the list.

Lack of politeness and manners can have profound effects on the performance of whole teams and organisations. If you fail to demonstrate basic civility, the consequences can be dire. Research published in *Harvard Business Review* shows that there is 'rampant incivility' in most organisations. The study argues that politeness contributes positively to people's morale, commitment, performance and sense of wellbeing.

Civility requires restraint, respect and responsibility in everyday life. Without these, you can never act ethically. I believe good manners are here to stay – they're an essential part of social and business culture. You *will* be judged by how polite you are.

I am happy to share with you that I have been won over by manners during the interviewing process. While it might seem shallow to be swept away by common courtesy, what it really shows is consideration, kindness and respect. I know our fast-paced, technology-driven environment makes us so used to our digital communication shortcuts and speed. Add to this the frequency with which we are working from home, which mounts up to less human-to-human interaction and a loss of social skills. So, use your manners to stand out – both when job seeking and working.

The hardest job kids face today is
learning good manners without seeing any.

–

FRED ASTAIRE

Six simple courtesies

1. Stand up when your interviewer enters the room.
2. Give a firm handshake with consistent eye contact.
3. Send a follow-up email or say thank you verbally.
4. Respond to emails promptly and with full sentences.
5. Use salutations and proper sign-offs.
6. Smile.

Looking after yourself

The transition to full-time work can be tricky. There will be adjustments required as you acclimatise to full time employment. Think of it as work jet lag – it just takes longer to adjust! It may sound trite, however the change to your life is significant, so it's worth being prepared.

Full-time work is a totally new experience: you have no work friends, you are out of your comfort zone, possibly a little scared, you do not know what is expected of you or what the norms are.

So, you need to look after yourself and get organised with good habits and rituals.

Sleep will be your number-one tonic. In the beginning you are likely to try to catch up your sleep by lying in on the weekend. It took me 20 years to realise this was counterproductive and added to the torture of Monday mornings. Try and have adequate sleep and go to bed at roughly the same time each night if you can. It will assist you with healthy routines.

Making exercise part of your life is critical to maintain balance and relieve stress. It will help you to be more optimistic and have a healthy outlook on life and work.

Regular exercise facilitates:

- improved cognition and concentration
- sharper memory
- faster learning
- prolonged mental stamina
- enhanced creativity
- lower stress.

Please do not confuse me for your parent, but like sleep and exercise, what you eat is important. I recommend taking your lunch and snacks to work, for two reasons:

1. Buying lunch every day is expensive!
2. It will assist with making good food decisions.

Organisation is essential for survival. A week of full-time work will leave you exhausted, especially in the beginning. Sunday nights are your secret weapon for surviving Monday morning. Have your clothes organised for the week ahead –laundered and ironed in advance. Clean your shoes, remove or redo your nail polish and trim your beard. Think about how you want to look when you arrive at the office in the morning, and prep as much as you can so you won't be rushed. Scooting in just on time with wet hair gives the impression that you don't care much about yourself, let alone your job.

***

This early stage of your career will no doubt have its challenges, but I hope it is also an inspiring and happy time for you. Put the work in now and you reap the rewards of a fulfilling and fun career.

TOP FIVE TAKEAWAYS

1. Do take a part-time or casual job while you study – it counts.
2. Remember it's a numbers game and you have to be in it to win it.
3. Guard your reputation and check your social media.
4. Give yourself extra time to prepare for and settle into your first job.
5. Manners, always manners!

9

When life gets in the way

Four days will quickly steep themselves in nights;
Four nights will quickly dream away the time.

–

WILLIAM SHAKESPEARE

This chapter is all about midcareer. You may be at the Advancement stage – moving along a career path, reaching goals and either going on to greater heights or perhaps levelling off. Or you might be in Maintenance – maintaining productivity, perhaps mentoring someone less experienced, evaluating your career goals and even contemplating the kind of legacy you would like to leave behind.

As I mentioned in the introduction, for the first time ever the workplace now caters for five generations. With increased life expectancy and tenure in the workforce, 'midcareer' may mean late 50s for some. However, typically at midcareer you will be in your early 30s to late 40s.

There is a certain freedom in reaching midcareer. For one thing, no-one is going to ask you what you want to be when you grow up!

You have the pleasure of asking that same question and seeing the awkward familiarity in the expression of the person you're conversing with as they tell you of their future dreams. As for your dreams, they've either become a reality by now, or you have invented new ones along the way.

The 30s and 40s are a time of mixed emotions. It can be a crossroads for your career and employability. It can also be a time when you question your future direction, and when life inevitably gets in the way of your carefully mapped out path.

In this chapter we will examine the challenges of midcareer life. We'll look at:

- the positives of being in this age group
- how to survive life's scrum
- how to avoid dropping the ball
- career malaise and how to turn it around
- being sacked (fired) or made redundant.

YOUR 30s AND 40s – YOU HAVE IT ALL!

In some ways, when you're in your 30s and 40s you have it all. You have bundles of experience, both in work and life, you're young enough to still have energy and bounce, and you have acquired many varied skills. You can still enjoy the youthful parts of yourself but you're old enough to appreciate your maturity and acquired wisdom.

You also have knowledge, maturity, tolerance, confidence, self-efficacy, better boundaries and coping abilities, resilience, patience, better listening skills, increased EQ and better control of your emotions. You are most likely across most aspects of technology, if not the latest.

Research shows that as you age, you're more likely to use your emotions for problem-solving – particularly if you're a woman.

As you reach your 30s and 40s you will possess a better understanding of yourself. You'll be more self-aware and have a longer track record – your own biography. With your increased self-awareness comes the gift of appreciating your journey, honouring your achievements and accepting people (and yourself!) for who they are. By now, you have likely learned what you can and can't change about yourself. You appreciate your limitations, and you are better at managing your energy, time and intentions.

All of this says you are at your prime in terms of employability. Leverage it! It's a wonderful age to take it all!

According to career researcher Douglas T. Hall, the middle career stage can occur at different times depending on the person. He defines midcareer as a time when you have attained a level of achievement and established yourself in an occupational or career role. However, if you change careers several times or have time away from work (to care for children, for example), you might dip in and out of midcareer several times.

LIFE'S SCRUM

And then there is life: that thing that can get in the way of your best-laid and intended plans. Marriages, divorces, mortgages, family, health issues, ageing grandparents and parents are all the reality when you're at this age. You may be in life's scrum, head down and attempting to gain back possession of what you once had. You're experiencing competing priorities of career, family, promotions, additional study, longer hours, possible relocation, extended travel, even being made redundant or sacked. These are life's givens.

You may have started to have health concerns or be dealing with other people's health issues – your parents', for example. You have no doubt also experienced death or tragedy in some form and the halcyon days of your youth might seem a world away.

When the pressure starts to build at this point in your life, something must give. It might be your health (physical or mental), your relationships, your family or, in a lot of cases, your employability. It's entirely natural, with all these competing pressures, to simply stop 'investing' in your employability. Often, for couples, it will affect one person – and that person will see the dreams, ideals, drive and ambitions they once had losing their significance and place in life. If neglected for too long, this is when your employability can be at risk.

In some cases, unforeseen events may force you to redefine your future goals completely and take on a new career path. You might reinvent yourself, emerge as an entrepreneur or tap into a creative pursuit with great success. Vera Wang was a figure skater and journalist before entering the fashion industry at age 40. Today she's one of the world's premier women's designers. Donald Fisher was 40 and had no experience in retail when he and his wife, Doris, opened the first Gap store in San Francisco in 1969.

Just because you have reached midcareer doesn't mean you will necessarily coast through to retirement. It's never too late to make a change in your career.

DON'T DROP THE BALL

It's easy to take your focus off the goalposts when you have so many conflicting priorities. However, with just a little effort it is possible to keep working on your employability at this stage of your life.

Keep it fresh!

Some people become 'old' quickly. I interview people and catch up with friends, and sometimes it feels like they are racing to retire. I am not suggesting hanging onto your youth inappropriately, but you can be fresh and current and nurture and love the inner child in you long into mature age (whatever that is!) Age is an attitude, and positive, youthful energy goes a long way to increasing your employability.

Embrace technology

Technology will keep you current. Set aside time to keep up with the latest advancements in your field, so you don't go down that slippery slope of becoming tech ignorant. It can happen quickly, and you may not even realise it!

Tech incompetence will age you more than your spritz of grey hair. Secondly, it will impinge on your credibility – the credibility you have spent 20-plus years building! A couple of poorly executed Zoom calls can be enough to set the tone. Okay, perhaps I am exaggerating now, but you have all seen that person I am referring to. Help yourself and work hard to prevent that being you.

Despite the cliché, there is no reason why older people can't embrace technology. When Facebook was first launched in 2004, it was created for university students, but who is on Facebook now? The 20-somethings from 2004 – who are now in their 40s – and their parents. At 60-plus, plenty of people are picking up the skills to use technology. It just takes a bit of effort. Tech isn't hard, its incremental.

CAREER MALAISE

At this midlevel stage, you have acquired experience, established credibility and have a certain level of authority, regardless of your seniority and leadership. According to executive coach Whitney Johnson, one of the biggest reasons for midcareer dissatisfaction is boredom. By the time you're in your 30s and 40s you know what you're doing, and you miss the 'dopamine rush that comes with learning and achieving.'

If you're opting to take a simpler job to accommodate lifestyle changes or adjusting priorities, the price might be the loss of motivation and some boredom. It's the quid pro quo.

Boredom is linked to a decrease in motivation. Being bored at work will affect your career and employability. And, if you're not careful, you can slip into this mode quite easily, without even noticing. Research published in the *Journal of Career Assessment* acknowledges that 'job boredom is a common experience at work' and suggests that finding meaning in your job is one way to conquer this.

So, what should you do if you're feeling lacklustre about your work? Here are my suggestions:

- Continue to learn. This need not be a commitment to a degree – there are other ways to keep learning. Be proactive and ask for feedback so you can work out your development areas (don't wait for your annual performance review to do this). This will give you something to focus your learning on.
- If you're able to commit to it, ask for a promotion or what you need to do to earn one.
- Consider a lateral move or secondment.
- Put your hand up for special projects or company activities outside of your division or department, even if it's simply to be more social at work.
- Take on a mentoring role.

All these activities will put you in a position of continual learning and provide you with meaning – an essential ingredient for countering boredom. Longer, prolonged scenarios and situations are best, although even a shorter online course or webinars will be beneficial.

When you first delve back into learning, you may go through a stage of adaptation where you're rebuilding your confidence and warming up these learning muscles. Starting with short courses might help here, as they allow for a slower and more comfortable pace.

To counteract boredom, your mind needs to be stretched, probed, provoked, intrigued and explored. Learning is supposed to be challenging, so dive deep into an intellectual enquiry that resonates with you.

If you are 40-plus, don't waste all that experience you have acquired and skills you have learned – leverage them. You have come too far to go backwards now.

SACKED OR MADE REDUNDANT?

If you've been in the workforce longer than 10 years, chances are you have experienced being sacked or made redundant. It's also likely to happen to you again before you retire. So, if this is something you are going through, join the club!

Although they are different experiences, both termination and redundancy can be deeply traumatic. The feeling and impact are similar, and both require considerable reflection, strong awareness, regrouping and moving ahead.

Being sacked is one of the worst employment situations to be in, no matter your role, level or circumstances. This is true even if you may have been expecting to lose your job, or didn't like your job anyway. The 'rejection' pill is hard to swallow. You may feel shame, embarrassment, anger, humiliation, anxiety and fear. All these emotions are legitimate. Once you feel and acknowledge these emotions, it is all about how you chose to deal with them. The step towards action and resolution will decide whether you stay 'stuck' or turn the situation into a new opportunity.

Does being sacked or made redundant make you unemployable? Absolutely not.

What happens after you're fired or made redundant depends on your attitude. Your challenge will be harder, as you will need to explain the situation to prospective employers, but I am sure you recognise that already. This is when your reflection and self-awareness need to be on point – to handle this sensitive situation in the right way and avoid it having power over you.

Firstly, let's look at what *not* to do. Do not make things worse. Avoid the temptation to complain to your ex-colleagues about the situation, and most certainly do not vent on social media. Also, if you can, hold off on interviewing for a new position until you can be rid of any emotional baggage associated with being let go. How long this takes to process will vary from person to person and in some instances, you may never forget it, but you will learn to leave it in the past. However, you need to be in a position where you can discuss or talk about what happened without resentment, anger, bitterness or the urge to be passive aggressive. It may be hard, I know!

Once you are calmer, reach out to your boss or HR to receive some constructive feedback about your performance at work, if possible. Its brave, confronting and will require courage and perhaps some swallowing of your pride, but it's worth it to receive feedback. If you are surprised by the situation you are in, you need to understand what happened. Being surprised may mean you overlooked something essential, and you may need to reflect and ask yourself what led you to ignoring the signs and clues.

Most importantly, you need closure. Being brave in situations like this and acting with dignity will help you to repair and move on.

If going to your boss or HR isn't an option, try a trusted colleague – but tread with respect. Listen, do not debate or argue and thank them for any feedback, insights and observations they share with you.

If there is really no way for you to collect feedback, you must be brave and honest with yourself. Take stock of the situation and ask your own best friend (that is you, by the way). Be honest with yourself to understand what happened and the role you played.

Take responsibility, wholly. Dig deep to come away from this in a better place. It will likely be confronting.

Remember earlier in the book when I described my own redundancy? Yes, it was a redundancy rather than a termination, but afterwards, I also recognised that I was not an ideal employee. I did not like my job and was disengaged. I would have made me redundant as well.

So, how aware are you of your shortcomings and development areas? Do you have old performance reviews you can go through? Look for patterns. Read between the lines and look for the invisible ink.

During the global financial crisis (GFC) of 2007–08, I had to make 70 per cent of my team redundant. It was traumatic for them, and for me. One of these employees reached out to me afterwards to ask for feedback. It was genuine. I was surprised she did this and thought it was brave of her. She has since excelled in her global career and I am still in touch with her today.

Ultimately, if you're facing termination or redundancy you need a plan. Now could be the time to look at different career paths and opportunities. Five career changes in a lifetime is the average for Australian workers. Maybe now is the perfect time to be inspired and get creative.

***

The challenges specific to the midcareer demographic are legitimate. However, a cautionary message: do not use these challenges as a crutch. Your challenges are no different in magnitude to those faced by school leavers or retirees. Keep agile, fresh and focused. Be accountable and responsible for your own future and career.

We lack real role models in today's world. As someone who is not a celebrity, but a real person with a story to tell, this is your opportunity.

TOP FIVE TAKEAWAYS

1. If you're bored with your job, make a list of the things you'd like to learn and action it.
2. You are in your prime – leverage it!
3. Tech is incremental.
4. If you've been let go, you need a plan.
5. Think of yourself as a role model, and act accordingly.

10

Parents returning to work

I thought about quitting,
but then I noticed who was watching.

–

UNKNOWN

Being employable connects with your whole world. After returning from parental leave, this is especially true – you need to manage the often-conflicting priorities of family and work life. However, just because you are returning from parental leave and have other priorities does not mean you need to accept a soulless job, or a job that may not cater for your newfound needs and responsibilities.

At EST10, we deal with this issue daily. When I'm working with a parent returning to the workforce, it feels as though my job has morphed from recruiter to trusted counsellor. The number of return-to-work parents seeking advice and guidance on current market conditions is increasing, as is the length of time parents are now choosing to stay at home with their children.

That said, some of the very best candidates I have met have been returning to the workforce after five-plus years (or even longer). The keys to success every time have been a great attitude, patience, flexibility, commitment and keeping up-to-date with technology.

In this chapter we'll work through some of the tricky issues facing return-to-work parents. We'll investigate:

- the changes in the workplace you're likely to face
- how to apply for a new position
- the importance of technology
- the need to embrace flexibility.

WHAT WILL I GO BACK TO?

Continuity is important for your employability as well as your well-being. When you have left your job for a specific time, even for a joyous occasion such as a birth, the continuity is broken. Your job may be waiting for you, but there is still worry and concern. Will you find the same culture, people and environment you left behind? Also, with your baby's arrival, you are not the same person – how will your colleagues adjust to this?

Chances are you will not go back to the same old. The world is changing daily, and so are businesses, in small and significant ways. Leaving for parental leave or any other reason requires significant adjustment.

If you have never been on parental leave or had time away from the workforce, you may wonder what the big deal is. The truth is, it can be emotionally and psychologically brutal, causing you to question the very core of your self-belief.

Parenthood often feels like a new identity, especially if it is your first experience. You start describing yourself as a mother or a father, rather than in terms of your former solo identity or profession. According to Daisy Wademan Dowling, founder and CEO of

Workparent, returning to work after being home with a new baby is 'a transition that's like no other'. Everything changes, she says, 'from your practical day-to-day schedule, to your new responsibilities as a parent, to your identity in terms of how you've seen yourself your entire adult life.'

At EST10, we have seen a shift in the length of time people are taking from work as parental leave. It is no longer six to 12 months – it's often 18 months to two years and even, in some cases, until children go to school. Our employees at EST10 have always taken more than 12 months, and more than half decided to take extended leave beyond two years to see their children off to school. The longer you are away from work, the more concerned you may be about what you are coming back to.

The workplace has evolved considerably in recent years, most notably due to rapid advances in workplace technology. The introduction of wi-fi, mobile devices, teleconferencing and videoconferencing and, most recently, global health concerns requiring us to work from home have all transformed the way we conduct our business. Hot-desking and activity-based working environments were becoming more popular prior to the pandemic, and now working from home is the norm in some cases.

Not surprisingly, these changes have shifted the traditional parameters of office-based roles. Today, being able to work with technology is more crucial than ever.

These days, companies are often a little less prescriptive when it comes to the nine-to-five workday, opting for earlier or later starts and finishes depending on industry and client needs. All of this can work to your advantage if you are returning to work, but it can also be a disadvantage if not treated in the right manner. Personality and habits can play a significant role here. Some people thrive better in a more structured environment, and some are less reliant upon others to stay motivated. If you're working from home, the right protocols will still need to be in place as if you were working in the office:

focus, respect of deadlines and motivation will continue to matter. The traditional office environment assists with the structure of this, so don't be surprised if you struggle with this adjustment at first. Many of us do!

From the files

One return-to-work candidate that sticks in my memory for all the right reasons is Deborah. Her résumé could have stayed among the hundred or so other applications we received for the role she applied for. Instead, she called us straight after sending her application through. This proactive approach is not very common in current times, since online submissions are the norm. Deborah had been looking after her children at home for 12 years. I spoke with her and she oozed a beautiful positive energy and can-do approach. Because she had kept herself up-to-date, she was tech-savvy.

I tested the ground with her, explaining the difficulty of someone entering the workforce after this period of time. I told her she would need to be flexible. However, it was clear that this would not be a problem for her. She demonstrated a great attitude and full understanding of the reality of her situation.

I mentioned that she would need to do some skills testing for us. 'Sure,' she said, 'I'll do it tonight.' And she did. This further assured me I was dealing with a responsible and willing individual. I was in love from there and knew I could assist her – because she was making it easy for me to do so. We were in it together.

By the following day I had arranged a job interview for her. It was a last-minute interview slot and not convenient. She had to juggle the children's pick-up times from school, but she made it happen and took it on as her issue to sort, not mine. She paid for parking, placed her children in a cafe downstairs with a friend and attended her interview on the floor above.

She only needed to attend one interview because she was offered the job. She is still with the organisation in a higher-level role. Deb is adored in that organisation. Why? Because she has a great attitude, a fresh approach and is up-to-date with her skills.

Being current with her skills gave her confidence. She knew she had been out of the workforce for a long time but did not feel disadvantaged or that she couldn't find a job – all because her technical skills were on point. Deb didn't forget the skills, know-how and nous she had developed when she was last in the workforce 12 years prior, either. She did not think twice about calling us to follow up on her job application, because that is what was done 15 years ago. It still works.

APPLYING FOR A NEW POSITION

Depending on your circumstances and the length of time you've been on parental leave, you may not be returning to the job you had before – you could be looking for a brand-new position. We cover résumés and interviews in part III, but there are a few additional points to add that are specific to those returning from parental leave.

Before you even start your job search, do your research. I suggest partnering with one trusted recruitment consultant who can provide you with an in-depth understanding of current market conditions, workplace cultures and salary expectations. You also want to choose the agency that sees you in the right light and invests generously in the time you deserve.

When you work with an agency, they will be your advocate and cheer squad, helping you get your application across the line in the same way I did for Deborah.

As recruiters, we always want to assist everyone in finding a job. However, we have limited time to invest despite our best wishes. It is not about choosing between 'deserving' and 'undeserving' candidates, but instead choosing to champion those we believe in, who believe in themselves and, most importantly, who need someone to believe in them. When you find all of that in a person, you are not just doing your job – you are giving parts of yourself that go far beyond simple recruitment.

Whether or not you partner with a recruitment consultant, there are a few key aspects to focus on when you're preparing to apply for a new role.

Get on board with technology

Technology is forever changing, and rapidly so. You will have a greater chance of securing employment if you are across and comfortable with new technology trends. Not only will you have the skills but, more importantly, you will be confident and at ease when talking about them in interviews.

Make sure you're up-to-date with the technology relevant to your industry. Research the latest workplace software tools that may have replaced old systems. There are hundreds of online courses now available, many of which are free. A good place to start is LinkedIn's learning pages; the University of Sydney also offers some great information technology courses.

Update your résumé

It goes without saying that you'll need to update your résumé. Chapter 12 will help with this, but I have some special tips for more mature job seekers, too.

First, make sure you include any new soft or technical skills you have developed. Some employers assume that parents who have been out of the workforce for a long period of time are less skilled, or that their skills have become rusty. This is a myth you will need to dispel, both within your résumé and at interview.

As you will know more than anyone, managing a household with children fine-tunes problem-solving, organisational and time-management skills, and is one of the best environments to develop resilience and innovative thinking. You are also witnessing and supporting your child's development, which gives you greater observation abilities as well as increased patience.

Delve into your experiences and draw out examples:

- What skills have you gained that make you more competitive?
- What can you deliver?
- What will you be good at?

Also, highlight any volunteer experiences and subsequent skills you have gained while out of the paid workforce.

When updating your résumé, ensure your LinkedIn profile matches. Additionally, it needs to be a professional 'five-star profile'.

Also, your phone voicemail message – is it professional? The same goes for your email address. Nothing lewd please! You want to stand out for the right reasons.

Be flexible and prepared to hit the ground running

Be ready to work. Have your childcare already sorted. You will make it harder for your interviewer or recruiter to assist you if they are presenting opportunities or even job offers and you are unsure of when you can start because your childcare isn't organised. They may perceive you as being disorganised, a tyre kicker, even entitled. It may even cause them to move on to the next candidate. Only go to market when you are ready to return to work psychologically and practically.

Do not restrict yourself to permanent opportunities. Consider contract roles as well. Contract roles can open up permanent roles within an organisation, provide great networking opportunities and are invaluable for your résumé as a return-to-work parent. This is also valuable if you need a period of adjustment.

As an indicator, at EST10 close to 50 per cent of those we place in temporary or contract positions find permanent work in the organisation we place them in. The permanent roles are not necessarily at the same level we placed them in, either – they are other roles found within the organisation.

When you start applying for new roles:

- Be available to easily take a phone call. Expect to interview quickly.
- Expect a video interview of some sort, so be across Zoom and the like well before the day of your interview. You don't want to be frazzled on the day because you can't work out the mute button.
- Try your best to accommodate the proposed interview times.
- You need to have already taken care of your family commitments in the eventuality you secure a role immediately. School pick-ups and relevant childcare arrangements need to be in place, at least tentatively, so you are ready to commit as soon as possible. The expectation will be that you can start straight away or within a standard four-week timeframe.
- Lastly, be enthusiastic! Be dedicated and committed to making your new career chapter work for you, your family and your new employer.

***

If you're returning to the workforce after a period out of it, thinking and planning well in advance is key. Your mind needs to be across the transition, so you can 'see' yourself at work. What areas do you need to work on, such as getting across new technology, before you start applying for roles? What logistics do you need to figure out? This should all be sorted before you even start to think about writing your résumé. Your confidence may still be a little fragile, but all these actions will have you well and truly on the pathway to securing a role and continuing your employability.

TOP FIVE TAKEAWAYS

1. Accept your new identity and embrace the challenge.
2. Be aware that your workplace may have changed considerably while you've been absent.
3. Have all the logistics, including childcare, sorted before you apply for a new role.
4. Make sure your tech skills are up to scratch.
5. Try to be flexible and think of this as a new adventure.

11

To retire, or not?

I must be careful not to get trapped in the past.
That's why I tend to forget my songs.

–

SIR MICK JAGGER

As you mature, retirement and health become the two most important topics – the source of hope and anticipation, but also stress and worry. It is a time to look back, feel proud of the fruits of your labour and make plans for all the experiences you want to enjoy but haven't had time for earlier. However, as many experts point out, retirement can also be one of the most stressful periods of your life.

Retirement can be an unspoken and uncomfortable topic for various reasons. The issue of retirement presents itself when you approach 'retirement age', but what if you would prefer to keep working after this designated age? Whether it be for financial reasons or you simply enjoy working, many of us are reluctant to give up our working lives.

In this chapter we'll look at employability in our later years. We'll examine:

- the psychology of retirement
- the current employment landscape
- how to be employable at 'retirement age'.

THE PSYCHOLOGY OF RETIREMENT

While some people arrive at retirement feeling happy and joyful, this is not the case for all of us. Dr Robert P. Delamontagne, author of *The Retiring Mind*, says, 'People go into retirement essentially flying blind.'

In his research, Delamontagne found people often aren't mentally prepared for the retirement transition and don't fully grasp what it will mean for their identity and place in the world. He says, 'People can go through hell when they retire and they will never say a word about it, often because they are embarrassed.' He says the cultural norm that retirement is living 'the good life' means that people who have a different experience feel forced to remain silent.

Australians have a combined life expectancy today of 83 years and, like most developed countries, this is increasing. We don't have a fixed retirement age – we become eligible for the age pension at 65.5 years of age at the time of writing (rising to 67 by 2023), and our access to superannuation varies.

Australians are increasingly working to older ages and are the fastest-growing section of the workforce. In 2018, 13 per cent of Australians aged 65 and over were working, compared with 8 per cent in 2006. Only a very small percentage of mature employees I meet nowadays are retiring because they want to.

Psychologically, there is the important factor of feeling valued and contributing to society. For many, your career becomes part of your identity. So how do you navigate giving it up?

Like most challenges in life, the key is to have some control or power in the decision-making. A crucial part of the solution is to be employable, no matter your age. If you look around, there are plenty of people making their careers work for them later in life:

- George Miller AO is a 76-year-old Australian film director, producer, screenwriter and physician best known for his Mad Max franchise. In 2016 he was nominated for Best Picture and Best Director for *Mad Max: Fury Road* at the Academy Awards.
- Ita Buttrose AC, OBE is an Australian journalist, business-woman, television personality and author. In 2019, aged 77, she became the new chair of the Australian Broadcasting Corporation (ABC).
- Julia Child worked in advertising, media and secret intelligence before writing her first cookbook when she was 50, launching her career as a celebrity chef in 1961.
- Michael Bloomberg left his job as CEO of financial software, data and media company Bloomberg LP at 59 in 2002 to assume the role of mayor of New York City, which he held for 12 years. He then re-assumed his role at Bloomberg, before running in the 2020 US presidential election campaign.

THE EMPLOYMENT PLAYING FIELD

Pre-COVID-19, Australia was already in the midst of a significant talent shortage, giving candidates a greater opportunity to be considered for roles. Labelled the 'war for talent', the shortage – across all job categories and disciplines – meant all employers were looking at their criteria, requirements, who they employed, how they employed and their expectations. Diversity and inclusion rightfully have been hot items on all managers' and HR leaders' agendas. According to researcher Justine Irving, 'Ultimately, older workers are a key element of a diverse workforce. Diversity of workers in an organisation, including a mix of younger and older workers, ensures breadth of experience, skills and knowledge from which to meet the varied needs of consumers.'

Post-COVID-19, we are facing yet another talent shortage – this one fiercer than before, as the readjustments and rationalisation from our COVID-19 experience emerge. A considerable portion of Australia's candidate pool have indicated a preference to opt out of the workforce or seek part-time positions post-COVID-19. Many of these people lost their jobs or had reduced hours imposed upon them, or at best needed to work from home. People have become acclimatised to the new world and, as a result, are finding new priorities. For some – more than 30 per cent, according to the research conducted from our office – the preference is to spend more time with their family. The statement often heard now is, 'we can survive on one or a reduced income.'

In addition, Australia is also seeing a reduction in immigration and skilled workers. In May 2020, Prime Minister Scott Morrison estimated around 34,000 people would migrate to Australia in 2021 – a far cry from pre-coronavirus estimates of around 270,000. Looking further ahead, it is predicted there could be 500,000 fewer people in Australia in 2040 than previously predicted.

We're now living longer, too, so you may feel you are able to squeeze in a few more years of work without missing out on your retirement years. Since 1900 the global average life expectancy has more than doubled and is now above 70 years.

All this reads well for anyone at 'retirement age' who is not wanting to retire. There are genuine opportunities for you. More so, our economy needs you. Believe it!

BEING EMPLOYABLE AT 'RETIREMENT AGE'

As I mentioned earlier in the book, for the first time, Australia's workforce includes five different generations:

- Generation Z (born 1997–2012)
- Millennials (born 1981–96)
- Generation X (born 1965–80)
- Baby Boomers (born 1946–64)
- Silent Generation (born 1928–45).

This is something quite fascinating to witness and be a part of. How do you coexist, compete, add value and ensure your employability at a time in your life when you may be feeling your most vulnerable?

The elephant in the room is the perception of being 'old'. You cannot change your wrinkles and grey hair, but you can change your outlook to be one that is fresh and 'youthful'. Perception is the way in which you are being seen or viewed. It may not be your intention to be perceived in a particular way, but it could still be someone else's reality of you. That said, you can do your best to change people's perceptions of you. Working on your confidence and self-esteem will assist you in feeling positive, optimistic, happy and sure of yourself, giving you the confidence to present in the manner you want to be perceived.

Confidence and self-esteem

Regardless of your role, if you are nearing 'retirement age' you bring a wealth of experience and knowledge to the workforce. There's no doubt you know your stuff! What I often see in older applicants, however, is self-doubt and a lack of confidence. For some, it seems there is a tipping point – the more experience and knowledge they gather, the less confidence and self-esteem they possess.

If you are feeling insecure, work on regaining your confidence and self-belief. In the early stages of your job search, start thinking back through your years of experience. Go to the vaults of your memory and become so familiar with everything you have done that it's almost like a broken record (but your favourite record!). You need to know what you know and be able to articulate it with confidence.

Start with a 'long bio'. Think of it as a very long résumé, similar to the master résumé we talk about in chapter 12. Start from the beginning, but concentrate on the last 20 years. Capture each role: title, tasks, projects, all achievements, wins, challenges, to whom you reported and so on. Consider how you felt in each role. Channel that feeling and keep it, for this will help jog your memory and assist with your confidence during the interview. The long bio is just for you, so there are no rules. It can be as long as you like. You can write it in diary form or stick to a résumé style or even bullet points.

The process may not be quick and that's okay. The purpose is to refamiliarise yourself with your skills and experience, as well as build your confidence, self-efficacy and self-esteem. It will happen the more you think and write, and I hope at the same time, this process will reaffirm how amazing you are! As you go about everyday life – attending to the needs of your family, walking the dog, driving, catching the bus, cleaning, gardening – reflect on all your experiences and then write them down! Make a commitment to do this daily.

When considering your skills, think of both hard and soft skills. The soft skills are key, as these are usually finessed and fine-tuned with time – this can be your competitive advantage. Start to think of and position yourself in this way, in terms of your competitive advantage – what you offer versus your counterpart. Remember, your fellow interviewees might be a lot less experienced than you!

Knowing your competitive advantage will go a long way towards ensuring your confidence in the application process and interview.

Attitude

I am going to call a spade a spade here and at the same time, give you a gift: the deal-breaker for anyone interviewing or applying for a job is a poor attitude. You may be scared, feeling unconfident, or uncomfortable that after all these years you are being 'judged'. These are all normal emotions, but it will not benefit you to be perceived as defensive during the interview. Quite the contrary – it may cost you the opportunity.

When you are confident, it is unlikely you will feel the need to be defensive. I have met too many 'older' candidates with such great experience, however in the interview they have a 'front' that is contrary to how I know them genuinely to be. I always think of Robert De Niro in the movie *The Intern*. When I am in my 70s this is the person I want to be in the workforce: kind, composed, helpful and wise, with a great attitude.

Networking

Don't be uncomfortable networking. It doesn't have to be a case of attending an awkward event where you're forced into small talk. It could be as simple as reaching out to those you know to let them know you are looking for work. It's well known in recruitment that between 50 to 80 per cent of jobs (or even more) are found via the candidate's own network. Opportunities can come from people the candidate hasn't had contact with for years, so it is worth reaching out to your 'dormant' connections, too. Networks are powerful. Do not underestimate the fact that people want to assist.

Being part of professional associations is another way to increase your network. Not only will it keep you up-to-date, ensuring you have depth and not just surface understanding, but it will also provide you with benchmarking, market updates, knowledge of who's who in your space, peers, support and possible opportunities.

Being current

Being current will be your most significant advantage. This is the one area that people *expect* to be your downfall. The associations you are a part of will assist in your knowledge being current and relevant for your industry. You will also need to be up-to-date with technology, news, cultural trends and views. Be brave, get across all new technology – it will build your confidence, keep you mentally agile and assist in securing a job that works for you!

From the files

A very close client of mine, a senior banking executive, lost his job in the recent COVID-19 fallout. In fact, his entire team of executives were all made redundant. The difference between the rest of the team and my client was his age – he was 60. Despite the shock, he didn't mope around and he didn't let his ego get in the way of progress. Instead, he just got moving – literally.

Firstly, he made himself go for a walk every morning (great for discipline, optimism and self-motivation) to set himself up in a routine. The walk got longer and longer, and before he knew it he started walking to places he used to drive to.

As he relaxed, his mindset then became one of exploring, not rushing. When he went to the local grocer, he spent time chatting. When he went to his local boutique wine shop, he spent longer chatting. This man loves his wine (a lot!) and spent most of his 'chatting time' in this shop.

One day, the wine shop owner was stuck: the delivery guy didn't show up. So, my client, an ex-senior banking executive who previously was on a significant salary, started helping out the owner with his deliveries. He found that he loved chatting to the people he was delivering to, suggesting wines and increasing the shop's sales. The shop owner and the ex-banking executive are now discussing a new business venture together.

Here's another example. When the GFC hit in 2007–08, the fallout was significant. A very close friend of mine, who was edging towards 60 at the time, had a very successful education business. He floated his business as the GFC occurred. His business was wiped out, and significantly so – houses, boats, cars, everything, even his wife – all gone.

Deciding what to do next, he used his own experience to identify gaps in the market. He ended up starting a bespoke chauffeur business, providing a service he wished he'd had as an executive. He would take all his friends, business contacts and former colleagues to the airport, events or wherever they needed to go – like a taxi, but with an executive touch. Punctuality became his number-one competitive advantage. He developed strong and trusted relationships with pre-screened back-up drivers who could take on jobs if he was too busy or caught in traffic. If that was to be the case, he then made sure to call each customer as a follow up on the service provided by the backup driver. It was simple, but no other driver provided that level of service, let alone the champagne in the boot, mints, water, newspapers, door opening and so on that became standard for his service. He even got to know his regular customers' choice of coffee and made sure he had it ready for each morning's pick up.

My point is you cannot stop moving and doing. A challenge like this will take you to the next place and the one after that – eventually, to the place you want to be. Be open to exploring new options or doing something totally different. Do you have a hobby that you can turn into a job? Now's the time to take action.

Age is just a number.

–

GEORGE FALLON CALDER (MY DAD)

Be a perennial

In recruitment, we are seeing a global trend that the previous rules and norms of retirement have been thrown out the window. As we've already touched on, people are working longer and there is greater acknowledgement that 'life' extends well beyond the age of 65. Older adults are defining themselves by their mindset and attitude, rather than their age. There's even a new term for such people: perennials! I think we'd all like to be a perennial: someone who keeps on growing, year after year, and bouncing back after every setback.

While we have to acknowledge that prejudices, stereotypes and biases exist when it comes to older and more mature employees, there are also examples of businesses worldwide tackling this subject and doing things differently.

While as an older person you may not be able to perform in certain labouring types of jobs as you did when you were younger, some companies are utilising employees in these categories in many other ways and in different sorts of capacities, with great results.

There is also a trend in some retail companies to employ more mature staff, as these companies rightly see older employees as possessing strong interpersonal skills and positive, warm attitudes.

However, even when businesses have programs and strategies in place to encourage older workers, you, as a mature employee, will still need to be employable, regardless of the incentives and support available.

The good thing is that your experience will have given you an abundance of transferable skills and attitudes that you can use in a range of contexts. These include:

- **Wisdom:** life experience cannot be learned from books, and this is where mature employees have an upper hand compared with younger people.
- **Patience:** you are probably more patient, with less of a need to be competitive in general.

- **Willingness to share:** you may be more giving of your knowledge, experience, information and life's lessons.
- **Mentoring skills:** you may be a 'nurturer' and enjoy giving as a mentor.
- **Interpersonal experience:** you have already worked with every possible type of co-worker and manager and know how to handle them. Your perceptions of others, as well as your understanding of people's behaviour, is deeper. You may also have travelled the world and dealt with more people from different backgrounds, which helps in understanding and appreciating differences in the workplace.
- **Reliability and responsibility:** you have built the right work ethic over a long period of time and can be relied upon to meet expectations.

Cognitive abilities

Many people think that older people's cognitive abilities are dwindling. Medically this might be true, but there is also evidence that this might not affect people's abilities at work in the way you assume. According to HR experts Josh Bersin and Tomas Chamorro-Premuzic, the scientific evidence shows that 'for most people, raw mental horsepower declines after the age of 30, but knowledge and expertise – the main predictors of job performance – keep increasing even beyond the age of 80.'

***

If you want or need to keep working past 'retirement age' there are so many ways to make this happen. Yes, stereotypes exist, but these do appear to be breaking down over time. All evidence suggests that if you embrace the positive aspects of ageing – the vast experience, skills and wisdom you have acquired during your career – there is no reason why you can't continue to have a happy and fulfilling work life well past the age of 65.

Go get 'em!

TOP FIVE TAKEAWAYS

1. Be aware of the psychological hurdles you're facing as you age.
2. Take comfort from the fact that your skills and experience are needed in the current employment landscape.
3. Work on your self-confidence – this is often what is standing in your way.
4. Remind yourself of everything you are good at and have achieved.
5. Watch *The Intern*, and be Robert De Niro.

PART III

The employable toolkit

If the only tool you have is a hammer,
it's hard to eat spaghetti.

–

DAVID ALLEN

THIS IS THE practical part of the book. We will now dig deep into the toolkit you need to assemble to be ready for anything – whether it's starting out, seizing an opportunity, advancing your career or switching careers.

The quality of the tools you employ during your job search and the application and interview process can make or break your career. What a shame to work on your personal and professional growth by developing the 7 attributes, only to be let down by a substandard application. It would be like having the most perfect and beautiful house to sell, but no sales agent or advertising.

Think of yourself as a brand. Everything you do during the hiring process should reflect that brand – from how you lay out your résumé to how you word your cover letter, how you answer your phone to what you display publicly on your social media, how you present for your interview to how confident your greeting is.

This part of the book will help you to:

- write a killer résumé that is targeted, relevant and well presented
- stand out from the crowd with a cover letter that gets your application to the top of the list
- land that job you always wanted with your professional interview skills.

12

Custom-build your résumé and cover letter

There are no shortcuts to any place worth going.

–

BEVERLY SILLS

Your résumé and cover letter are key tools in your employability toolkit. They should showcase your employability. The writing skills you display in your résumé and cover letter will have a major impact on your job search, so it is also well worth developing these skills and making sure your application demonstrates them. When it comes to your résumé and cover letter, think of the expression 'first impressions count'.

The purpose of a job application is to connect as quickly as possible with the people who are in a position to hire you. Your chances of an employer reading your application and beginning a conversation with you increase dramatically with a personalised, well-crafted cover letter and résumé. These are the first impressions an employer will have of you – and first impressions are everything when it comes to your résumé. You would be surprised just how many candidates put themselves forward for positions, especially those that are the most interesting and competitive. Standing out for all the right reasons is key.

In this chapter we'll take a deep dive into the world of CVs, résumés and cover letters. We'll look at:

- the structure of a CV and a résumé
- how to create a master CV and turn it into target résumés for each job you apply for
- seven tips for a great résumé
- the role of artificial intelligence
- how to write a compelling cover letter.

CV OR RÉSUMÉ?

You may be wondering, what is the difference between a CV and a résumé? Although the terms are used interchangeably in Australia and the US, we'll differentiate them here.

Traditionally, a CV is a longer document. It is named from the Latin *curriculum vitae* – the course of one's life. It includes everything you've ever done and can be edited according to the relevance to the job you're applying for to make a résumé.

Leonardo da Vinci was considered as the first person to write a résumé in 1482.

A résumé – from the French *résumé*, meaning summary – is just that: a summary of your relevant experience and skills.

I recommend your résumé to be up to three pages, or possibly up to five if your relevant experience extends to 30 years or so.

GET NOTICED FOR THE RIGHT REASONS

Recruiters, whether internal or from an agency, are very busy and seem to be always time poor! This means if you want to be 'seen', you must ensure your application is easy for the recruiter to digest. Your résumé and overall application *must* be tailored to the job brief or advertisement, or even the job description if you have access to one.

Make sure your résumé is easy to read. When reviewing résumés for a job vacancy, I may have 200 applications to consider for each role. I don't want to miss out on the perfect applicant by spending time I don't have on those who just won't fit. That means sorting applications quickly. With my well-honed skills tailored over many years, it takes me less than 20 seconds to scan each résumé – sometimes, under 10 seconds! If there are spelling mistakes, a cluttered layout and irrelevant information, this application may not go any further, let alone to the shortlist. Yes, this is tough news to hear, but all seasoned recruiters have the skills required to zero in on these details quickly.

A tailored résumé is one that will make me pay attention. Sending the same document for each job application is a recipe for failure. Consider this: with job applications now online, it is really easy for people to send applications for every job opening at the click of a button. The idea behind this action is: 'Oh, you never know, it might work.' These 'chancers' clog up the portal for the serious, well-matched applicants. I would strongly recommend you avoid applying for random jobs – not just for the sanity of recruiters like myself, but for yourself. Job hunting is hard enough, and you are creating additional psychological trauma for yourself by applying for jobs based on chance alone – much like buying a lotto ticket. Apply for jobs that are left of centre, by all means, but do so with a plan and strategy and follow-up, rather than leaving it to wishful thinking. Applying for jobs should never be like sending a message in a bottle into the sea of the unknown.

Employers are looking for someone who stands out, so sending standard information that you have not tailored to the job on offer lowers your chances. Your best chance of making a great first impression is ensuring that you tailor your résumé to the role you are applying for.

CREATE YOUR MASTER CV

Tailoring your résumé, as simple as it sounds, is a time-consuming process, especially when you are applying for multiple roles. If only there was a way to simplify the tailoring process...

Well, it turns out, there is! If you've never heard the term 'master CV' before, prepare to revolutionise your thinking when it comes to the job-application process. The master CV is one of the best time-savers there is.

Your master CV contains everything you've ever done: education; part-time, full-time and voluntary work; work experience; projects; interests and potential referees; as well as your skills, duties, achievements, tasks, strengths and more.

Each time you start or end a role, you populate this document with your experience. Over the years, you compile one really, really long document that keeps everything in the one place. This is very similar to a traditional CV, but more extensive in that you might include examples of projects you worked on, or other achievements that you might forget later down the line.

Your CV may run up to 20 pages – way too long to submit for a job application, but the idea is to edit a copy for each job application, tailoring it to fit into one to three pages.

Make sure you are always employable: diarise updating your master CV every month. Capture new projects, responsibilities and achievements while they are fresh in your mind.

Four benefits of a master CV

1. **Cuts down application time:** take the burden out of résumé writing by compiling every single thing you do in your job in your master CV as you go along.
2. **No more forgotten information:** how many times have you cursed yourself, after the fact, for not remembering that one great example the application asked for?
3. **Quick and easy progression check:** a master CV is a great way to take a big-picture look at your career. Ask yourself: 'Am I heading in the right direction?' You'll find it's much easier to answer this question if you can easily track your movements and progress.
4. **Great point of reference for interview preparation:** when you have landed an interview, you'll need to revisit your past experience in order to practise answering the behavioural/competency questions that are bound to come your way. Keeping all your experience in one place is by far the easiest way to jog your memory.

Most importantly, though, never submit your master CV to an employer! Use the information in your master CV to create target résumés: short, focused versions of the CV that are crafted specifically for the role you are applying for. You may have multiple target résumés for various job types, industries or clusters, which saves time if you are applying for several roles at the same time.

If you are working with a recruitment agency to find you a role and have a strong relationship with your consultant, I suggest sharing your master CV with them, so they have a full picture of your experience and potential. However, if you have applied for a specific role via a recruiter, you will have to tailor your master CV to a target résumé specific to that job opening.

Many companies have moved away from receiving résumés and are using their own application forms. This encourages candidates to tailor their application to the company and that job opening, rather than recycling the same résumé. If you have an up-to-date master CV, you can simply cut and paste the relevant information straight from there.

STRUCTURING YOUR RÉSUMÉ

Depending upon your role, your résumé can take a couple of different formats.

The first style is to list your previous jobs in chronological order. You would include the company, job title, tenure and your achievements, tasks and duties. If using this format, be careful not to repeat similar duties and tasks for every role. Typically, duties and tasks can be listed in a bullet style, which is easy to read.

An alternate style of résumé is to use the STAR format: situation, task, action and result. This style quantifies your duties and achievements. For example:

- **Situation:** what was your role?
- **Task:** what was the objective of the role?
- **Action:** what did you do?
- **Result:** what was the outcome of your actions?

The advantage of a STAR style of résumé is that it is very specific, and will help recruiters and hiring managers to assess your previous position duties and past achievements quickly. It will bring your achievements and capabilities to life.

SEVEN TIPS FOR A GREAT RÉSUMÉ

Your résumé is potentially the most important document you could ever write, so it deserves serious thought and consideration. These seven tips are a great starting point. I've included a sample résumé, figure 12.1, so you can see how it fits together.

1. Avoid using buzzwords

In 2014, US job site CareerBuilder released a survey of recruiters' and hiring managers' most unappealing buzzwords to see on a résumé. According to Rosemary Haefner, VP of Human Resources at CareerBuilder: 'Subjective terms and clichés are seen as negative because they don't convey real information. For instance, don't say you are "results-driven"; show the employer your actual results.'

Here are the top 10 terms that made the 'worst résumé terms' list:

1. Best of breed
2. Go-getter
3. Think outside of the box
4. Synergy
5. Go-to person
6. Thought leadership
7. Value add
8. Results-driven
9. Team player
10. Bottom line.

2. Skip the career objective

The career objective is the statement at the top of your résumé stating your occupational goals. Too often it's a fluffy statement that doesn't add much value. If this is the case, then it's best to leave it out. If you do want to include a career objective, focus on your progression and keep it short and to the point. For example: 'After three years in a junior PA role, I am looking to develop my skills in an EA role, with the view to support at C-suite level in the future.'

3. List your professional development and associations

Your professional accreditations and associations are key indicators of your passion for, and commitment to, your career and industry. They also demonstrate that you are proactive and want to be well informed about any changes and developments in your area. Always be on the lookout for professional-development opportunities and don't forget to include these in a separate section on your résumé.

4. Include full dates, not just years – and explain any gaps

When including your experience, start with your current or most recent position and work backwards. Provide full start and finish dates (including both the month and the year). Treat each promotion as a separate position. If you're following your boss to a new organisation, do mention it – it shows loyalty and assumed competence.

Most importantly, explain any significant career gaps. Even if you were not working, you may have picked up some valuable skills from other pursuits.

5. Aim for two to three pages, maximum

If preparing a target résumé for an employer, keep your résumé down to three pages or less.

If you have had a lot of jobs or a long career, you might want to focus on your last 10 years' experience, summarising roles earlier than that under a heading such as 'Previous employers' or 'Earlier career'.

You could also omit your earliest roles, giving readers the option to view these by including a line such as 'Full résumé available upon request'.

6. Ensure your LinkedIn profile, including job titles, marries up with your résumé

Most employers will check your LinkedIn profile at some stage. Consistency, congruency and transparency are key. Don't try to paint your responsibilities in a certain way if your LinkedIn profile shows something different.

7. Tee up your references

I always advise adding a section at the end of your résumé that says, 'References upon request'. It is best to get in touch with your references before starting your job search, to make sure they will be available and willing to be your referee. Psychologically, it also sets a good impression and might cause your referees to think about a great role for you – saving you the time of job hunting!

Figure 12.1: sample résumé

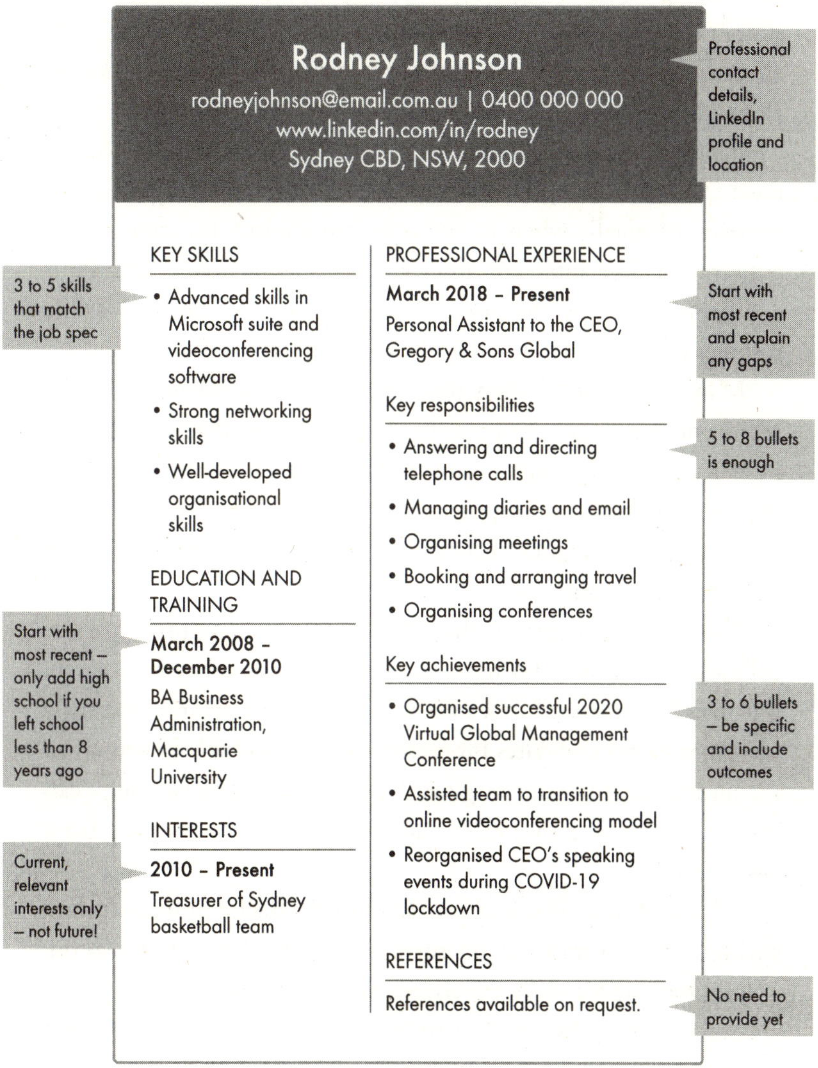

Rodney Johnson

rodneyjohnson@email.com.au | 0400 000 000
www.linkedin.com/in/rodney
Sydney CBD, NSW, 2000

KEY SKILLS

- Advanced skills in Microsoft suite and videoconferencing software
- Strong networking skills
- Well-developed organisational skills

EDUCATION AND TRAINING

March 2008 – December 2010
BA Business Administration, Macquarie University

INTERESTS

2010 – Present
Treasurer of Sydney basketball team

PROFESSIONAL EXPERIENCE

March 2018 – Present
Personal Assistant to the CEO, Gregory & Sons Global

Key responsibilities

- Answering and directing telephone calls
- Managing diaries and email
- Organising meetings
- Booking and arranging travel
- Organising conferences

Key achievements

- Organised successful 2020 Virtual Global Management Conference
- Assisted team to transition to online videoconferencing model
- Reorganised CEO's speaking events during COVID-19 lockdown

REFERENCES

References available on request.

ARTIFICIAL INTELLIGENCE AND YOUR APPLICATION

I'm often asked whether it is important to include particular keywords in résumés, and whether recruiters use artificial intelligence (AI) to scan and assess applications. The truth is, recruiters have been using AI for longer than most people would think! AI is simply the use of technology to assist with problem-solving. Like all technology introduced into work processes, it is designed to improve workflow.

For the most part, recruiters use AI for efficiency. One of the most time-consuming activities for a recruiter is manually screening résumés, especially when we are trying to identity the right candidate from a large applicant pool. The ease in which you can submit a job application via the internet means around 75 per cent of the résumés received do not match the requirements of the role.

Many candidates, when first hearing of the use of AI in the recruitment process, are concerned. They worry that without the human element they may be at a disadvantage. The truth is that you do not need to worry, because as a candidate, AI actually works *for* you, giving you a higher likelihood of being noticed, if you have the right experience and skills.

Around 75 per cent of the global workforce comprises passive candidates – those who have not yet begun an active job search, but may be interested in a new role. AI effectively and efficiently identifies these candidates for recruiters. AI can also help you if you are unsuccessful in your original application – the technology can track your career movements and place you in the pipeline for a future role.

AI also reduces bias and prejudice in the hiring process. It does this by ignoring information such as race, gender, age and so on, instead looking for skills, experience and attributes.

So, what does AI actually do? In screening résumés, AI will look for keywords, experience, industries and competencies that match with the job or profile set. This is why it is so important to tailor your résumé for each role you apply for. A generic résumé will likely not make it through.

A generic approach to résumé writing is a little like throwing mud and hoping it will stick. Job searching is discouraging enough, so it's far better to use technology to your advantage by doing the preparation beforehand in knowing the keywords, experience and competencies that and the job advertisement is calling for, and write your résumé accordingly.

THE RESULTS-ORIENTED RÉSUMÉ

Employers focus on skills and capabilities, not just particular job roles, so your résumé needs to reflect this.

Most people think writing up the experience section of your résumé is easy. After all, it is just a list of your roles and key duties, right? Listing your duties is a great starting point, but résumés that stand out from the rest use the experience section to tell a story rather than just providing a checklist. Consider the following examples:

- Example 1
  - Answer phone calls
  - Document preparation
  - Manage junior staff
- Example 2
  - Answered 20 client phone calls per day
  - Formatted 5 documents per week
  - Trained and supervised 10 junior staff

See the difference? It may not look like a big change, but quantifying your experience is one of the best ways to demonstrate your competency, showcase your past success and prove your suitability for your new role.

Writing an achievement-oriented résumé is easier than you think. Here's how it's done:

1. **List your duties:** your goal is to provide a list of bullet points concisely summarising your role. A great way to put together this list is to run through a normal day at work and keep a record as you go. Looking at your job description is also a great start, but if you've been in your role for some time, don't forget to look beyond this and include any new responsibilities that may have arisen over time.
2. **Look for action words:** the next step is to start turning your bullet points into short phrases. Rather than starting with a passive opener like 'I was responsible for' or 'I worked on', consider an action word like 'managed', 'implemented' and so on. This makes you the initiator of the action, not just someone who blindly followed a job description. If you're struggling to find verbs, a quick Google search will give you more than enough to get you started.
3. **Add in numbers and results:** a simple tally of the number of times you completed an activity within a given time period is the simplest way to quantify your duties, but some duties may not be that easily quantified. If that's the case, look for other metrics. For example, did you increase sales or productivity by a certain percentage? Was one of your projects completed within a tight deadline? Did you work on an important project with a large budget?

If you can't quantify every line in your résumé, that's okay, but if you can quantify some if not most of your résumé, you are going to be able to tell a better story on paper than the candidate who just copied and pasted their job description.

THE VISUAL RÉSUMÉ

A visual résumé is one that uses infographics and other design elements to convey key information. Their use is on the rise, but should you adopt this style of résumé?

If you are in a creative industry, visual résumés have their advantages, but as much as you'd like to believe that a beautiful résumé can land you your dream job, the fact of the matter is that anything too different from the norm probably isn't going to do you any favours. Remember, hiring managers are time poor, so when it comes time to screen hundreds of résumés, any information that cannot be found within seconds is going to land that résumé in the 'too hard' pile. Yes, visual résumés are great at simplifying information, but because we're so used to purely textual résumés, reading them isn't necessarily intuitive. The best résumés strike the perfect balance.

My five favourite résumé design principles

1. **White space:** this is the space between the elements on your page. Put simply, the more content you put on your page, the less white space there will be. White space helps the reader to comfortably navigate your résumé. If your résumé is too busy or overly crowded, this disorganisation will transfer to the reader, encouraging a sense of confusion or ill-ease. Aim for a simple résumé design with ample white space.

2. **Colour:** but don't go overboard. Colour should be used strategically to create contrast between different sections and highlight important information. If you would like to add a splash of colour in your CV, I recommend sticking to one or two colours and using colour for smaller sections of text such as headings or subheadings.

It needs to look professional and smart, not like a colourful rainbow!

3. **Repetition and consistency:** this promotes cohesion. Done right, repetition will strengthen your résumé by bringing together its disparate parts. You might like to try styling all your headings in the same font or colour, keeping your tone of voice and tense consistent and ensuring that spacing between lines and paragraphs is the same.
4. **Balance:** this is as much about look as it is about feel. This can be tricky to master because there are no hard-and-fast rules about what constitutes a balanced résumé. Take a step back from the computer screen and get a feel for whether your résumé is pleasing to the eye. If something isn't right, it'll stand out immediately – you may want to rearrange your layout, ensure that each section aligns to an invisible grid or play around with the scale/size of your headings.
5. **Simplicity:** one of the things great designs often have in common is their simplicity. This goes for the colour and composition of your résumé, as well as its length!

SHAPE A COMPELLING COVER LETTER

A cover letter is often expected in a job application, although it must be said that recruiters and hiring managers do not always read them immediately. I normally go straight to the résumé to get a quick overview of the candidate's experience, and then return to the cover letter to help me fill in any gaps and obtain more of an insight into that candidate. So, while your résumé might be the first thing the hiring manager considers, your cover letter is also a very important tool that could clinch the deal and land you an interview.

Selling yourself with the written word can be a challenge, but it's worth persevering with. Most positions require excellent written communication skills, so proving you can express yourself fluently and concisely will enhance your professional standing. The exercise of doing this will also help you to articulate your 'why' at the interview with ease.

What to include in your cover letter

The purpose of spending time constructing a cover letter is to make your application stand out. It will demonstrate the following to the employer:

- that you have read the job description
- that your skills are relevant to the job
- that you could bring value to the employer.

As such, a generic cover letter is not going to do you any favours. Customising your cover letter to the role being advertised is imperative.

When crafting your cover letter, I suggest including a brief discussion of your job history (but not repeating your résumé) so if there are any queries raised from your résumé, your cover letter will answer those questions.

Focus on answering the following seven questions in your cover letter:

1. Can you do the job?
2. Do you have the right qualifications, knowledge, skills, abilities and experience?
3. Will you do the job well?
4. Are you reliable, self-motivated, agreeable and enthusiastic?
5. Are your values and goals a good match for the organisation you're applying to?

6. Will you make a good impression on clients and co-workers?
7. Do you have good written communication skills?

In your writing, make sure you mirror the values of the company you're applying to, using words and language similar to theirs.

I've included a sample cover letter, figure 12.2, for your inspiration.

***

I hope this chapter has provided you with the confidence to craft a tailored, thoughtful résumé and cover letter that will grab the attention of the hiring manager for all the right reasons. Before you submit your application, it's worth doing a final check to make sure you've addressed all the requirements that are specified. And, of course, proofread your work before submitting it. You'll be well on your way to securing a conversation with your dream employer.

TOP FIVE TAKEAWAYS

1. Update your master CV regularly so you can quickly and efficiently seize job opportunities as they come up.
2. Create a tailored, targeted résumé of no more than three pages for each job you apply for.
3. Quantify your duties, achievements and results.
4. Think visually in terms of design, white space and the way the text sits on the page.
5. Focus on answering the seven questions in your cover letter.

Figure 12.2: sample cover letter

Include your full contact details – address, email and phone number – and today's date.

Rodney Johnson
123 Smith Street
Sydney, NSW, 2000
rodneyjohnson@email.com.au
0400 000 000

26 March 2021

Address the hiring manager by their name.

Roxanne Calder
EST10 Recruitment
66 Hunter Street
Sydney, NSW, 2000

Dear Ms Calder,

Include the role title and reference number.

Re: Executive Assistant – 12345

I am writing to apply for the position of Executive Assistant to CEO at EST10 recruitment that was advertised on your website on 20 March 2021.

Inbox management and travel arrangement are essential to the executive assistant profession, and I can execute both effectively and efficiently to a high degree while maintaining the utmost discretion.

I have enclosed my résumé as part of my application and have highlighted below some key skills I can bring to this role:

List key skills and experience matching the job specification.

- Professional services industry experience: I have 10 years' experience working as an Executive Assistant with the last three spent supporting a CEO of an global management consulting company.
- Networking: Through my career I have built and nurtured key stakeholder relationships worldwide to support my executive.
- Organisation: This is a key attribute required to be an effective executive assistant, and one that I have developed through, among other things, managing an inbox with 200+ emails a day.

My skills and experience outlined will enable my success in the position of Executive Assistant to CEO and in becoming a pivotal part of the EST10 team.

Explain your interest in the company and role.

EST10 is a company I have been interested in since learning about your passion for the recruitment space. I would love to be a part of a culture that holds teamwork at its centre and focuses on personal development, as I have seen through your LinkedIn page.

Thank the hiring manager and include a call to action – what would you like to happen next?

Thank you for taking the time to consider my application and I look forward to hearing from you.

Warm regards

Rodney

13

Ace the interview

One important key to success is self-confidence.
An important key to self-confidence is preparation.

–

ARTHUR ASHE

I see exceptional – and I mean *exceptional* – people miss out on jobs, all because they didn't interview well. When I talk with them after the interview I can always tell exactly why this has happened.

I know the candidate *should* have secured the job, because I interviewed them myself, heard their stories, and witnessed their great values and merits, so I know they would have been a great asset. I also know the market and benchmarking, so am also not delusional as to the alternate talent available.

Why, then, did they struggle to convey all this in the interview? The number-one reason is nerves.

Nerves can trigger stress, making you unable to express yourself clearly and putting you at war with your internal sense of who you are and what you are projecting. When you succumb to nerves, you're likely to make the biggest mistake of all: saying what you think the interviewer wants to hear, rather than your real truth. Even if it is difficult to do, telling it how is – professionally – makes you genuine and authentic. You will be seen as trustworthy, and that is what people want in an employee and co-worker.

So, let's take a look at some tips and techniques you can employ to ensure you're calm, collected, and less likely to let nerves get the better of you. In this chapter we will cover:

- the importance of authenticity
- how and what to research before the interview
- planning your responses and questions
- how to walk into the room with a level of confidence you may be far from feeling
- special techniques for video interviews
- four mistakes that could cost you the job
- what to do after the interview.

THE RIGHT ANSWER IS AN AUTHENTIC ANSWER

Interviewing is an exploratory, honest, reciprocal conversation. The questions are designed to highlight what is essential to both parties – skills, qualities, values, attributes and fit.

Let's start by exploring why authenticity is so important to convey during an interview. Imagine you are in that all-important interview, and you are asked why you left a certain job. You might think a generic answer of 'it was just time to leave' or 'I'd learned all I could' is what the interviewer wants to hear, instead of your real answer which may be to do with the environment or cultural issues. Reasons concerning cultural issues are a challenge to portray in the right way, but it's far better to practise expressing that answer until you are comfortable with how and what you are saying than to provide a generic answer that you think is 'right'.

There are no right or wrong answers at an interview, as interviews are a two-way conversation. The only right answer is an authentic answer. This is when the interview and conversation can start to get real. Experienced interviewers see through generic answers and might assume you're using them because you have something to hide. It's such a shame when the majority of the time this is not the case – its just your nerves and good intentions getting in the way of an authentic response.

Before the interview, breathe, repeat positive affirmations about yourself and your abilities, and think of all the reasons why you would be perfect for the job and why you would employ you. Adopt this style of thinking and believing in yourself as a daily ritual and thought process. This will assist with your general self-esteem and confidence.

You can even admit to your interviewer how you feel – it makes you human!

Being authentic doesn't mean not caring about what you say or how you say it. It also doesn't mean that the interviewer has to 'fall in love with you' because you have been genuine. What it means is that you leave the interview knowing you have not betrayed yourself. That has the effect of bolstering your self-esteem and self-trust.

In a great interview, the interviewer can see what you have done, what your potential is and what makes you 'you'. If you're authentic, you're more likely to convince them that you're the right person for their business.

Think of it this way: imagine you are looking for a flatmate. What is important to you: honesty, values, habits, attributes? That they pay rent on time, are clean, are a non-smoker, are honest and trustworthy? What questions would you ask? What are the generic answers, and what are the answers that resonate? A job interview is not too dissimilar!

When you're interviewing a potential flatmate, you know straight away if they have provided an inauthentic answer. And even if the 'real' answer isn't what you wanted to hear (they leave their wet towel on the floor regularly), I bet that, in being honest, they have given you the perception that they are trustworthy. Perhaps a trustworthy housemate is a good housemate, even if they do have some issues with their laundry maintenance.

There's another important reason to be authentic in your interview: if you're honest about a situation, it may be that the interviewer realises you would not fit with what is required of that role. It's far better that is identified early on. It also doesn't mean this is the end of the road for you. If you're honest, authentic, professional and likeable, you may very well open other opportunities and roles for yourself if not the role you have already applied for. The interviewer may know of another role in the organisation that would be a better fit for you, or have a friend of a friend who is hiring. This is how the world of recruitment works!

DO YOUR RESEARCH

If you have secured an interview, you are at the pointy end! Now you need to be game-focused and not leave anything to chance. It's showtime!

It is likely up to five other candidates may also be at interview. However, if the interviewer is particularly skilled at screening it could be down to just you and one other – especially so in a talent-constricted market.

At this point, your level of preparedness could be the difference between securing or not securing the job. Being prepared will also give you confidence on interview day, helping to stave off nerves.

Find out all you can about the company and position you're applying for. Use as many different sources as possible. A Google search will bring up the website, any media mentions and social media pages. Go beyond this – delve and uncover. Find any news articles from the last 12-plus months. Find out the name of the

CEO, chairperson and other relevant people in the department you're applying to. What does the company stand for? What are its values and ethics? See how this resonates with you and try to incorporate it naturally into your responses during the interview.

If you have the names of the people who will be interviewing you, research them. Check out their backgrounds, previous places of work and so on. You might even find you have mutual connections!

Give yourself the insider's advantage. Use your well-honed communication skills to uncover the real skills, traits and so on needed for the role. You can do this by carefully reading the advert and any job descriptions you have been given. Look for any words that are not used but you would have expected to see. Notice any traits listed as 'ideally' or 'preferred'. I also suggest looking up the profile of the incumbent on LinkedIn – that can show you a lot! How does your experience compare?

PLAN YOUR RESPONSES

It's a good idea to plan your responses to common questions you expect to be asked. These include:

- Why do you want to work here?
- What interests you about this role?
- What are your greatest strengths and development areas?

Practise your responses using the STAR method (situation, task, action, result) and link to your skills and accomplishments. Think of your achievements, adversities and challenges. Remember to plan authentic responses – not what you think your interviewer will want to hear. You may like to practise with a friend or partner or practise out loud.

Beware the humblebrag

Imagine that you're coming to the end of what has been a pretty amazing job interview. By sheer luck, it looks like you may just get away with not having to answer one of the most universally dreaded interview questions. But alas...

'What is your biggest weakness, or area for development?' the interviewer asks.

If you've ever stressed over how to answer this question, your concern is warranted. As with most interview questions, there is no clear-cut right or wrong way to answer. However, one tactic does not work: the humblebrag.

A humblebrag is a seemingly modest or self-deprecating statement intended to draw attention to something you are proud of. There are times where the humblebrag can come in handy, but if your response to the weakness question is that you are 'a workaholic' or 'a perfectionist', the only thing you may demonstrate is that you don't take self-reflection seriously.

As much as we'd like to deny it, everyone has weaknesses and that's okay. No-one expects perfection. What an employer is looking for when asking this question is proof that you are self-aware.

Here are some ideas so you have an answer ready:

- an area where you could improve or an area you are working on
- a past mistake and the steps you took to avoid repeating it
- anything that demonstrates introspection – this is far better than giving the impression that you're infallible.

At the end of the day, you are going to make mistakes. What matters most is your ability to learn from them.

PLAN YOUR QUESTIONS

As I mentioned earlier in the chapter, the interview is a two-way process. You'll be expected to ask questions, and these are a great way for you to obtain further information about the company and role. Consider what is important to you: the style of management, reporting lines, systems used, culture, values, further education, work-life balance. What are deal-breakers for you? Make sure you find out about those before you move on to the next stage.

Some further tips on asking questions:

- During the interview, focus on what the interviewer is saying so you don't ask them to repeat something they've already covered.
- Steer clear of questions that you should have found the answer to in your pre-interview research.
- Avoid asking about salary (see the next section) or taking time off.
- Concentrate on the company's approach to professional development or how they measure success.

WHAT ABOUT SALARY?

It's my rule of thumb to leave the discussion of salary until after the first meeting. Most people find it a tricky subject and all good communication cues go out the window, affecting your tone, energy and the atmosphere. It is better to position the very best version of you and let the salary discussion come later. However, if the salary is not in the job description and there's a possibility it may come up during the interview, it's worth looking into what equivalent positions are earning, and also consider your bottom line. A good plan is having three figures in mind:

- $xxx Delighted
- $xx Satisfied
- $x Bottom line.

WHAT TO BRING WITH YOU

If relevant, prepare some examples of your work to bring with you. Also pack a pen, the job advert, a notebook and a copy of your résumé.

Plan *not* to bring anything that is irrelevant to the interview: gym bag, groceries, a coffee or any beverages, sunglasses on top of your head, your lunch, earphones or books.

It's fine to bring your phone, but make sure it's tucked out of sight and switched off.

PLAN TO BE ON TIME

Recently I was asked in one of our masterclasses on interviewing whether it's ever okay to be running late for an interview. My answer? *No!*

Luckily, there are wonderful apps now available to plan your journey, whatever the mode of transport. Aim to get there 10 to 20 minutes early, just in case. In a few cases, being late can be justified, but it is a classic deal-breaker, so I always recommend giving yourself as much time as possible. Plus, rushing to the interview is likely to make you even more nervous.

If you do happen to be late, don't become stressed – but do acknowledge it and apologise (just once, not 10 times!).

PLAN YOUR OUTFIT

Crafting the perfect office wardrobe can be daunting, let alone for a job interview when first impressions are everything. Please do not let anyone sway you by saying what you wear to an interview is not important – it is. You are not going to a party or to the beach. You need to dress appropriately and match the occasion.

Dijanna Mulhearn, author of the renowned *Wardrobe 101* book series, has frequently been a key speaker at EST10's events, advising on attire. Dijanna recommends sticking to simple colour schemes and subtle prints for an interview. Outfits that are too bright and busy will often encourage that 'hot mess' look you don't want to portray. Select colours to suit your natural colourings, as well as the season. Using colour like this can have a subliminal effect, not just on others but also on your own psyche.

Have your outfit prepared well in advance – don't wait for the night before. Check if it needs dry cleaning or laundering, whether there are rips or missing buttons, and that it still fits. Most importantly, make sure you still feel confident wearing it.

POWER UP WITH A POWER POSE

In 2010, US social psychologist, author and speaker Amy Cuddy and two colleagues sought to measure the effect of power posing on two key hormone levels: testosterone (dominance) and cortisol (stress).

> **A power pose increases the amount of space you take up in the room ... think hands-on-hips and standing tall, like a superhero.**

Half the participants were asked to stand in a high-power position (expansive, with open limbs) and the other half were asked to stand in a low-power position (slouched/guarded, closed limbs). After two minutes, testosterone and cortisol levels were measured and compared to pre-pose levels.

The high-power posers experienced a 20 per cent increase in testosterone (dominance) and a 25 per cent decrease in cortisol (stress). The low-power posers experienced a 10 per cent decrease in testosterone (dominance) and a 15 per cent increase in cortisol (stress).

So, what does this mean?

Granted, it does sound ridiculous, but science proves that it works. Standing like Wonder Woman or Batman for two minutes before your job interview might just help you land the job of your dreams. Not only does it hardwire your brain to exude confidence and competence, but it also decreases pre-interview stress. As you consider yourself posing, it may also put an involuntary smile on your face, and that can't be a bad thing!

Just before your interview, find two minutes in a secluded area to channel your inner superhero before you head into reception. You will be even more unstoppable than you already are.

Your energy is always your first impression.
It is the foremost perception others will have of you.
This initial energy introduction is a calling card
you cannot fake.

–

ANTHON ST MAARTEN

WHEN THE INTERVIEWER IS LATE

So, we've covered lateness when it comes to you, the interviewee, but what should you do if the interviewer is late? It's easy to say we shouldn't apply double standards, however I like to preface my advice by asking myself, 'What would I be saying if this were my mother, sister, best friend?' In that context, my answer would be to wait patiently for as long as you can. You have so much more to gain than spending (wasting, even) your time feeling offended.

When faced with stress and uncertainty, you may be prone to behave impulsively and potentially make mistakes. You are also more likely to allow your emotional responses to cloud your judgment, causing you to experience your 'waiting' as a reason to be upset.

The bottom line is, becoming annoyed and impatient will likely affect your interview performance. So instead of becoming upset, ask yourself, 'How much do I want this job?' It's worth considering that the interviewer may have a legitimate reason for being late.

Don't be tempted to text your friend or partner about how late the interviewer is – this will only carry over to your body language and affect a range of biological responses. Read the paper or a magazine, or silently meditate, breathe, feel good and recite positive silent affirmations.

Wait for the interview, do well, receive an offer and then make the call on whether the interviewer's lateness was an issue.

Be patient. Patience is the mother of all virtues.

–

HRITHIK ROSHAN

VIDEO INTERVIEWS

COVID-19 has upped the chances that you will be required to complete your interview via video. As one of Sydney's leading admin-recruitment agencies with a London-based consultant, EST10 has long used Zoom or Skype as an effective interviewing tool for candidates. Here are some top tips of how to prepare for and present well in a video interview:

- **Check your connection:** technology is wonderful, but it can let us down at the worst moments. Log in well before your interview and check that everything is connected, especially your microphone and speakers – a silent interview is not a good interview! If possible, do a test call with a friend to get your volume and camera angle correct.
- **Practise your gaze:** don't focus all your attention on your computer screen. It's important to gauge the interviewer's response, but it's not engaging for them. Instead, alternate your gaze between the on-screen image and your computer's camera. This will appear to the interviewer as though you are maintaining eye contact and looking directly at them.
- **Prepare the area:** you don't have to think about your surroundings when you go to an in-person interview, but

on video you definitely do! Interviewers don't want to see your dirty dishes or unmade bed. Set up your computer pre-interview – check your camera angle and find a blank wall or sparse background to use as your backdrop.

- **Think about lighting:** if your light source sits behind your head, you are going to cast a shadow over your face. Instead, aim for a soft light in front of you.
- **What's that noise?** Interviews are normally held in private rooms with peace and quiet for both parties to speak and think. Ideally, a video interview should be no different.
- **Make sure you are not going to get interrupted:** think children, housemates or pets.
- **Check your appliances:** noises you wouldn't normally notice become loud and distracting on video. Turn off your TV and radio and avoid putting on a load of laundry or dishes until afterwards.
- **Present yourself properly:** it is easy to be too relaxed in a video interview because you are in your home environment. Sit as though you are in an interview room – this will not only portray the right image, but also help you prepare mentally.
- **Dress appropriately** – and yes, head to toe, even though your interviewer will likely only see your shoulders (better safe than sorry!).
- **Organise what you'd normally take to an interview:** have, for example, a pen, a notebook and a printed copy of your résumé ready on your desk. And remember: the interviewer cannot see what you are doing – let them know if you are taking notes so they don't think you are being inattentive or rude.
- **Have you phone off:** out of sight and reach!

- **Allow enough time** – video interviews are just as detailed and comprehensive as face-to-face interviews, so be prepared for an extensive discussion about your experience and future expectations. Don't schedule another meeting straight afterwards – allow time for an in-depth conversation.
- **Have your questions ready.**
- **Don't be put off by brief time delays:** these can cause video discussions to flow less freely than face-to-face conversations.
- **Be polite:** make sure to allow the interviewer to finish speaking before you start your answer.

FOUR MISTAKES THAT COULD COST YOU THE JOB

Most interviewers don't expect you to sound perfectly polished or completely free of nerves, but they will notice if you make any of these five mistakes.

1. Not dressing to meet the company standards

Keep in mind the saying 'dress for the job you want, not the job you have'. The nature of your desired job will ultimately determine how you dress for the interview. If you're interviewing for a job as a personal trainer, you might get away with dressing casually. On the other hand, when interviewing with one of Australia's biggest law firms, you will need to dress professionally. It is always recommended to err on the side of conservative – you likely will not be penalised for being too corporately attired.

If working with a recruiter, ask them to give you an idea of the dress code of the workplace before your interview.

2. Not knowing your own résumé

Companies today are on the lookout for people who have embellished their résumé, so many will test your knowledge of your own résumé! If you do not have a good handle on what you've written down, you will trigger red flags. Employers expect you to speak articulately about your job history and any other information on your résumé. Remember, your résumé is the road map for the interview, so be ready to answer questions based on its content.

3. Not knowing what the company does

No-one expects you to have a full understanding of the company's proprietary business model, but they will expect you to know its major products, important clients and main values. If you lack knowledge of what the company does, it will be noticed.

On this note, you should be prepared to sell how you fit in with that company's overall plan.

4. Asking the same old questions

Some interviewers believe that the ability to ask questions is paramount. The more you can engage with the interviewer through thoughtful questions, the better your chance of making an impression and being offered the job. Not asking thoughtful questions – or, worse, not asking any questions at all – can give them a reason to cross you off their list.

AFTER THE INTERVIEW

Consider a follow-up with a phone call or an email – this will show your initiative and manners, and get you noticed. Reflect on the interview – check back over this chapter and see where you may have not come across as well as you would have liked.

If you are not successful, ask for feedback. And use it! Reflect and seek to learn from it, to improve for next time. This is positive, proactive thinking.

***

There are not many of us who can say they thoroughly enjoy the interview process, but I hope the insights I've shared in this chapter will help you feel prepared and calm those nerves. This will put you in the best possible position to shine bright on interview day, and give your interviewers an authentic impression of how employable you are.

TOP FIVE TAKEAWAYS

1. Be authentic. Always.
2. Prepare for the interview by researching the company and your interviewers.
3. Plan your wardrobe and transport. Gather what you need to take ahead of time.
4. Power up with a power pose before you walk in.
5. Rehearse answers and questions and keep the humblebrag out of the room.

14

Where to from here?

My favourite things in life don't cost any money.
It's really clear that the most precious resource
we all have is time.

–

STEVE JOBS

You are employable – that's 'where to from here'! Or, at the very least, you should have some plans in place to improve your employability. I hope you feel the same way as I do about this precious gift of employability that you have given to yourself.

Being employable will afford you more freedom. You will not be beholden to a job or role you do not enjoy. You will have the choice to move, change or stay – at your discretion, with free will and confidence.

In this climate where change is inevitable, if you are faced with a redundancy, downsizing or change in economic circumstances, your employability is your insurance. You will be covered. You may still face moments of being frozen and fearful, but your employability gives you power to keep moving forward.

The sense of freedom in being employable is a vital psychological factor, too. It should make you feel more comfortable and safer within yourself.

Although compromises are part of life, you may feel that with an employability attitude, you are a better version of yourself, and not just within a work environment. For, as we have ascertained, you cannot simply switch on and off your attributes!

Another crucial advantage of the freedom afforded through being employable is a better alignment of your values and beliefs with your job. If these values are not currently aligned, you may be looking for another position that suits you more closely. This kind of freedom might not have been available to you before, causing a lack of fulfilment or meaning – a common cause of job dissatisfaction.

Your job links and connects your whole world. You most likely spend more hours at work than with your family, let alone sleeping. Your job plays a significant role in all other parts of your life and is often taken for granted, and its impact on your life underestimated. I believe many of us neglect our employability.

Don't think of your job or career as a natural journey, defined by order and in which you are the 'passenger'. Be the driver. You can control where and how you want to go.

It is my hope that working on the 7 attributes will empower you not just at work but in enriching your everyday lives. As the boundaries between work and life become softer, your satisfaction with work influences every facet of your personal life.

After all, you do not stop 'living' while you work, nor stop 'working' while you live. Your identity is becoming more tightly connected to your jobs, titles and work, so you need to be careful that you are still defining yourself as an individual.

I don't mean to say that there will not be times of hardship, setbacks, challenges or questioning yourself once you become more employable – all of that is a normal part of everyday life and will continue. The difference is, you will become more comfortable as you work through each new challenge or obstacle. These challenges are there to keep strengthening and testing you.

As you work through the attributes, you will learn that the choices you make enable you to relinquish any burden or fear you may carry. They'll give you the confidence to make and have faith in your decisions.

REVIEWING YOUR PROGRESS

Here are my suggestions for a course of action once you have finished reading this book.

If you haven't already, respond to the 'reality check' questions at the end of each of the attributes chapters. Answer them just for yourself. After three to four days, respond to the questions again and note any differences in your answers from the first time. By the way, differences are good – they show your level of self-awareness is increasing. Differences can also mean you are letting go of thoughts and biases you may have been holding onto.

Then, rate your ability in each of the attributes from 1 to 10, with 10 being the highest. If you score 10, then you have already reached a level of mastery. If you scored less than 10, which is likely the case, you have confirmed that growth and learning is indeed an ongoing process.

For the results to be helpful and serve a purpose, be honest and real with yourself. Be brave and willing to put yourself out there, and perhaps even ask your boss or mentor to give you a rating as well. Where there are gaps or discrepancies of more than one point between where you have rated yourself and where your boss has rated you, ask for an example to better understand the difference. You may also find that their rating is higher than how you have rated yourself, as we are often hard on ourselves!

Then, over a three-month period, record each episode, incident, difficulty or challenge you encounter at work; you are looking for at least one or two of these each week. Don't just think about major episodes; small, minor incidents are incredibly insightful as well. At the end of each week, write down:

- **the issue:** for example, I missed an important deadline
- **the outcome:** for example, the stakeholder complained; relationship damaged
- **your observation and reflection:** for example, I didn't communicate to my manager that I was overloaded; in the future, I need to be upfront and perhaps ask for help prioritising my workload ahead of time.

At the end of each month, revise the past four to five weeks, looking for commonalities or a pattern. A story will emerge; this is exactly what you are looking for. It will help you figure out the areas you need to develop and improve upon. This will help you to build a development strategy, which is impossible when you're looking at isolated comments and information, as opposed to recognising established patterns.

Be persistent and patient with this exercise, as it can be very powerful – not just for your ability to properly reflect upon the findings, but in changing the outcomes positively and in the moment, not after the fact. Your awareness will increase, you will be present in situations, see the patterns, know your triggers and be less inclined to react to irrational impulses. You will navigate your process effectively as events unfold.

This style of self-reporting was introduced to me when I completed my MBA, and has held me in good stead since. I still do this today, but rather in the moment. I have become more adept and can catch myself and adjust my behaviour accordingly, most of the time! It has assisted with developing my awareness and perception, saved me from chasing other meritless options and helped me to intuitively future-proof my employability. The great thing about this self-report is it will help you to step back, evaluate and see the reality of each situation. It increased my confidence and opened my eyes to be a better manager, and helped me to secure bigger and better jobs.

Because I could see each situation for what it was, I could apologise or acknowledge when I was in the wrong or at fault, and I did. I continue to apologise when appropriate; it helps me remain comfortably humble.

SEEKING A TRUSTED ADVISOR

Have you enlisted a person you can go to for honest feedback? This could be a peer, boss or mentor. I suggest asking someone in advance, explaining the path you are on and what you are seeking, and ask if they can provide honest feedback – not clouded by emotions, desire to please or even fear of hurting your ego.

Receiving and giving advice and mentorship are valuable and enriching experiences. It is important to be grateful for every honest and direct piece of feedback you receive.

GOALS AND LEARNING

What do you want to achieve? Your goals can be based on incremental improvements or concrete, specific outcomes. With both approaches you can achieve your goals; it is the method that differs. Be specific with your goals, so you can look back at your plan/strategy, whichever approach you chose, and see your progress realistically.

Ongoing study of some sort is a valuable way to reach your goals, while also improving your confidence, self-esteem and self-efficacy.

When I studied for my MBA, the learning was incredible, but the self-belief, efficacy and confidence I obtained were what surprised and delighted me most.

***

I opened this chapter with the wise words of Steve Jobs because, for me, time is precious. Ultimately, it is what we all want. It represents freedom.

It's my hope that you'll use your employability to give yourself, and your family, freedom.

About Roxanne

Roxanne Calder is not your average recruiter. Her approach to work and life is to go deep and approach each challenge head on, and with heart. In managing and recruiting, she loves to see the potential in people. Uncovering their hidden qualities is her skill.

As the world picked up the pieces from the 2007–08 global financial crisis, Roxanne realised her long-held dream of launching her own business: EST10 was born in 2010. Roxanne's ability to stay the course – to learn, adjust, upskill and reinvent – is what made her business strong. When COVID-19 struck, she had those attributes to fall back on. Roxanne and her business came out stronger on the other side.

Roxanne holds a Bachelor of Arts from Monash University and a Master of Business Administration from the Australian Graduate School of Management at the University of Sydney. She feels privileged to have worked with and been mentored by some of the best in the industry, including Julia Ross, Geoff Morgan, Andrew Banks and Greg Savage.

In her global career, Roxanne has worked across Australia, the UK and the Asia-Pacific. Born in Scotland, she has lived in Africa, regional Australia and Japan. It was in Japan, at the very beginning of her working life, that she discovered her skill for 'seeing' people – looking for the clues to understand who they are and what they are really saying. It's a talent that has served and inspired her ever since.

Roxanne loves animals, music and books – in that order. She has an ambition to live on a farm and, in preparation, has a list of animals at the ready: Highland cows x 2, Clydesdale, Powerful Owl, Tennessee fainting goats x 2, donkeys x 2, Pallas's cat, swans x 2, bison x 2 and chickens, to name a few. On the weekends, you'll find Roxanne exploring Sydney's parks with her husband, Rick, and dog, Daisy (who is incredibly smart and part-human). She exercises religiously and has attended several Muay Thai training camps in Thailand (describing herself as 'likely the least talented participant').

Roxanne believes employability is insurance for your future. Her motivation in writing this book is to help others discover the freedom and confidence to be gained by developing the 7 attributes.

Acknowledgements

So many people contribute to a book and the sanity of its writer. I never knew that before. For that reason, I really hope I do justice in thanking and acknowledging everyone who has helped me!

I've enjoyed writing this book so much, despite my trepidation, nerves and lack of faith in myself at the beginning – in fact, most of the way through! It has been one of the most challenging yet rewarding experiences I have had, and for that, I am very grateful.

Firstly, the very patient, smart, kind and compassionate Lesley. Thank you for suggesting the book to me, and for your encouragement. Thanks for not taking on my idea of a green cover, nor my question of whether we really needed to include my name on the cover when we were looking for extra space.

Brooke – oh my goodness, lifesaver. Thank you for your editing; for politely pointing out things that weren't right, always in the nicest possible way, and for getting rid of the 'fluff'. You have a talent for communication and for understanding the psyche, personality and style of the person writing.

My whole team at EST10, who contributed patience, encouragement and occasional inappropriate jokes to keep me going. Thank you for giving me the time, freedom and peace to be able to write.

My dearest friend Lily. If not for you, this book would not have happened. You told me three years ago to write a book, and I said you were ridiculous. 'Who would read it?' I'm so pleased I have done it now. It's been the very best challenge and a great feeling to be well and truly out of my comfort zone. My goodness, I needed that! Thank you for your belief in me, and for working with me and providing encouragement and input. All those nights and weekends – I owe you a million lost wine nights!

Mr Savage – thank you for the introduction to Lesley, and for suggesting the book and believing in me and the opportunity.

Many, many clients and candidates have provided inspiration and their valuable expertise and insights. There are, however, three I would like to say a huge thank you to for their time, input and ideas: Guy Farrow, Helen Calladine and Corinne Alter.

Finally, my very patient Rick. Thank you for your unwavering support, belief and love – always.

References

Preface

Stanford University 2005, '"You've got to find what you love," Jobs says', news.stanford.edu/2005/06/14/jobs-061505.

Introduction

World Economic Forum 2016, 'The Future of Jobs: Employment, Skills and Workforce Strategy for the Fourth Industrial Revolution', www3.weforum.org/docs/WEF_Future_of_Jobs.pdf.

Accenture 2020, '5 Priorities to Help Reopen and Reinvent Your Business', accenture.com/_acnmedia/Thought-Leadership-Assets/PDF-3/Accenture-COVID19-Five-Priorities-To-Help-Reopen-And-Reinvent-Your-Business-v2.pdf.

Chapter 1

American Psychological Association 2003, 'Believing You Can Get Smarter Makes You Smarter', apa.org/research/action/smarter.

Truluck, JE & Courtenay, BC 2010, 'Learning style preferences among older adults' Educational Gerontology, vol. 25, no. 3, pp. 221–236.

Gladwell, M 2008, *Outliers: The story of success*, Little, Brown and Company.

Harvard Health Publishing 2019, 'The thinking on brain games', health.harvard.edu/mind-and-mood/the-thinking-on-brain-games.

Chapter 2

Covey, S 1990, *The 7 Habits of Highly Effective People: Powerful Lessons in Personal Change*, Free Press.

Chapter 3

Clarke, J & Nicholson, J 2010, *Resilience: Bounce Back from Whatever Life Throws at You*, Crimson.

Ostafin, BD & Proulx, T 2020, 'Meaning in life and resilience to stressors', *Anxiety, Stress, and Coping*, vol. 33, no. 6, pp. 603–622.

ScienceDirect n.d., 'Coping Strategy', sciencedirect.com/topics/psychology/coping-strategy.

Clifford, C 2017, 'Adam Grant: Resilience is the secret to success. Here are 2 ways to improve yours', CNBC, cnbc.com/2017/06/06/adam-grant-how-to-improve-resilience.html.

Hendriksen, E 2017, 'How to Build Your Resilience', Psychology Today, psychologytoday.com/au/blog/how-be-yourself/201709/how-build-your-resilience.

Fraser, A 2019, 'The Dark Side of Resilience', dradamfraser.com/blog-content/2017/12/7/the-dark-side-of-resilience.

Wang, Y, Jones, BF & Wang, D 2019, 'Early-career setback and future career impact', *Nature Communications*, vol. 10.

Chapter 5

Eurich, T 2018a, 'Working with People Who Aren't Self-Aware', *Harvard Business Review*, hbr.org/2018/10/working-with-people-who-arent-self-aware.

Eurich, T 2018b, 'What Self-Awareness Really Is (and How to Cultivate It)', *Harvard Business Review*, hbr.org/2018/01/what-self-awareness-really-is-and-how-to-cultivate-it.

Eurich, T 2017, *Insight: The Power of Self-Awareness in a Self-Deluded World*, Macmillan.

Goleman, D 2005, *Emotional Intelligence: Why It Can Matter More Than IQ*, Bantam.

Porter, J 2017, 'Why You Should Make Time for Self-Reflection (Even If You Hate Doing It)', *Harvard Business Review*, hbr.org/2017/03/why-you-should-make-time-for-self-reflection-even-if-you-hate-doing-it.

Chapter 6

Orth, U, Trzesniewski, KH & Robins, RW 2010, 'Self-Esteem Development From Young Adulthood to Old Age: A Cohort-Sequential Longitudinal Study', *Journal of Personality and Social Psychology*, vol. 98, no. 4.

Tracy, B 2012, *The Power of Self-Confidence: Become Unstoppable, Irresistible, and Unafraid in Every Area of Your Life*, Wiley.

MindTools n.d., 'How Self-Confident Are You? Improving Self-Confidence by Building Self-Efficacy', mindtools.com/pages/article/newTCS_84.htm.

Desmarais, C 2016, '11 Ways to Build Your Confidence and Appear More Attractive', Inc., inc.com/christina-desmarais/11-ways-to-build-your-confidence-and-appear-more-attractive.html.

Manson, Mark n.d., 'The Only Way to Be Truly Confident in Yourself', markmanson.net/how-to-be-confident.

Kaplan Professional n.d., 'What is confidence in the workplace important and how do I improve mine?', kaplanprofessional.edu.au/blog/why-is-confidence-in-the-workplace-important-and-how-do-i-improve-mine.

Lipman, V 2017, 'Why Confidence Is Always A Leader's Best Friend', *Forbes*, forbes.com/sites/victorlipman/2017/05/09/why-confidence-is-always-a-leaders-best-friend/?sh=58a7894f47be.

Seligman, M 2006, *Learned Optimism: How to Change Your Mind and Your Life*, Random House.

Chapter 7

The Foundation for Young Australians 2017, 'The New Work Order: Report Series', fya.org.au/wp-content/uploads/2017/07/NWO_ReportSeriesSummary-1.pdf.

Hmieleski, KM & Baron, RA 2017, 'Entrepreneurs' Optimism And New Venture Performance: A Social Cognitive Perspective', *Academy of Management Journal*, vol. 52, no. 3.

Centre for Optimism n.d., 'Optimism and Innovation', centreforoptimism.com/Optimism-and-Innovation.

Harvard Health Publishing 2008, 'Optimism and your health', health.harvard.edu/heart-health/optimism-and-your-health.

Sirois, F 2018, 'The surprising benefits of being a pessimist', *The Conversation*, theconversation.com/the-surprising-benefits-of-being-a-pessimist-91851.

Psychology Today n.d., 'Pessimism', psychologytoday.com/au/basics/pessimism.

Porter, E 1913, *Polyanna*, LC Page.

Ackerman, CE 2021, 'Pollyanna Principle: The Psychology of Positivity Bias', PositivePsychology.com, https://positivepsychology.com/pollyanna-principle.

Seligman, M 2006, *Learned Optimism: How to Change Your Mind and Your Life*, Random House.

Chatterjee, A 2020, 'Pragmatic Optimism', LinkedIn, linkedin.com/pulse/pragmatic-optimism-avik-chatterjee/?articleId=6669106242876776448.

Brescia University 2017, 'Interesting Psychological Phenomena: The Pratfall Effect', brescia.edu/2017/06/pratfall-effect.

Menon, AS & Priyadarshini, RG 2018, 'A study on the effect of workplace negativity factors on employee engagement mediated by emotional exhaustion', IOP Conf Series: Materials Science and Engineering.

Chapter 8

Statista 2020, 'Share of population who hold a bachelor level degree or above in Australia from 1989 to 2019', statista.com/statistics/612854/australia-population-with-university-degree.

Burgess, M 2017, 'One in three university graduates work in jobs unrelated to their study', News.com.au, news.com.au/finance/work/careers/one-in-three-university-graduates-work-in-jobs-unrelated-to-their-study/news-story/192aec4a81b673fcd004f9608a750c3b.

Universities Australia 2019, 'Career Ready Graduates', universitiesaustralia.edu.au/wp-content/uploads/2019/06/Career-Ready-Graduates-FINAL.pdf.

The Foundation for Young Australians 2017, 'The New Work Order: Report Series', fya.org.au/wp-content/uploads/2017/07/NWO_ReportSeriesSummary-1.pdf.

Harvard Health Publishing 2011, 'Giving thanks can make you happier', health.harvard.edu/healthbeat/giving-thanks-can-make-you-happier.

Porath, C 2018, 'Make Civility the Norm on Your Team', *Harvard Business Review*, hbr.org/2018/01/make-civility-the-norm-on-your-team.

Workplace Ethics Advice 2015, 'Civility, Ethics and Workplace Behavior', workplaceethicsadvice.com/2015/04/civility-ethics-and-workplace-behavior.html.

Hogan, CL, Mata, J & Carstensen, LL 2013, 'Exercise holds immediate benefits for affect and cognition in younger and older adults', *Psychology and Aging*, vol. 28, no. 2, pp. 587–594.

Friedman, R 2014, 'Regular Exercise is Part of your Job', *Harvard Business Review*, hbr.org/2014/10/regular-exercise-is-part-of-your-job.

Chapter 9

Atkins, P & Stough, C 2005, 'Does Emotional Intelligence change with age?', Society for Research in Adult Development Conference.

IResearchNet n.d., 'Middle Career Stage', career.iresearchnet.com/career-development/middle-career-stage.

Gillett, R & Feloni, R 2017, '19 Extremely Successful People Who Changed Careers After Turning 30', Inc., inc.com/business-insider/people-who-found-success-and-changed-careers-after-30-years-old.html.

Akhtar, A & Ward, M 2015, '25 people who became highly successful after age 40', Business Insider Australia, businessinsider.com.au/24-people-who-became-highly-successful-after-age-40-2015-6?r=US&IR=T.

Knight, R 2018, 'How to Beat Mid-Career Malaise', *Harvard Business Review*, hbr.org/2018/08/how-to-beat-mid-career-malaise.

Sánchez-Cardona, I, Vera, M, Martínez-Lugo, M, Rodríguez-Montalbán, R & Marrero-Centeno, J 2020, 'When the Job Does Not Fit: The Moderating Role of Job Crafting and Meaningful Work in the Relation Between Employees' Perceived Overqualification and Job Boredom', *Journal of Career Assessment*, vol. 28, no. 2, pp. 257–276.

The Foundation for Young Australians 2017, 'The New Work Smarts', fya.org.au/wp-content/uploads/2017/07/FYA_TheNewWorkSmarts_July2017.pdf.

Chapter 10

Dowling, D 2019, 'A Working Parent's Survival Guide', *Harvard Business Review*, hbr.org/2019/07/a-working-parents-survival-guide.

Chapter 11

Delamontagne, R 2010, *The Retiring Mind: How to Make the Psychological Transition to Retirement*, Fairview Imprints.

Chamberlin, J 2014, 'Retiring minds want to know', American Psychological Association, apa.org/monitor/2014/01/retiring-minds.

Australian Institute of Health and Welfare 2020, 'Deaths in Australia', aihw.gov.au/reports/life-expectancy-death/deaths-in-australia/contents/life-expectancy.

Hughes, D 2019, 'How golden oldies are boosting the workforce', Australian Financial Review, afr.com/work-and-careers/careers/how-golden-oldies-are-boosting-the-workforce-20190731-p52cjd.

Australian Institute of Health and Welfare 2018, 'Older Australia at a glance', aihw.gov.au/reports/older-people/older-australia-at-a-glance/contents/social-and-economic-engagement/employment-and-economic-participation.

Irving, J 2018, 'Age as an asset. Are we doing right by older workers?', Diversity Council Australia, dca.org.au/blog/age-asset-are-we-doing-right-older-workers.

Ryan, H 2020, 'Coronavirus means Australia won't meet migration forecasts for a decade', *The Guardian*, theguardian.com/australia-news/2020/jul/07/coronavirus-means-australia-wont-meet-migration-forecasts-for-a-decade.

Roser, M, Ortiz-Ospina, E & Ritchie, H 2019, 'Life Expectancy', Our World in Data, ourworldindata.org/life-expectancy.

Paychex Worx n.d., 'How to Manage the 5 Generations in the Workplace', paychex.com/articles/human-resources/how-to-manage-multiple-generations-in-the-workplace.

Freeland Fisher, J 2020, 'How to get a job often comes down to one elite personal asset, and many people still don't realize it', CNBC, cnbc.com/2019/12/27/how-to-get-a-job-often-comes-down-to-one-elite-personal-asset.html.

Bersin, J & Chamorro-Premuzic, T 2019, 'The Case for Hiring Older Workers', *Harvard Business Review*, hbr.org/2019/09/the-case-for-hiring-older-workers.

Chapter 12

CareerBuilder 2014, 'Hiring Managers Rank Best and Worst Words to Use in a Resume in New CareerBuilder Survey', press.careerbuilder.com/2014-03-13-Hiring-Managers-Rank-Best-and-Worst-Words-to-Use-in-a-Resume-in-New-CareerBuilder-Survey.

Fatemi, F 2019, 'How AI is uprooting recruiting', *Forbes*, forbes.com/sites/falonfatemi/2019/10/31/how-ai-is-uprooting-recruiting/?sh=52f69fe146ce.

Chapter 13

Torgovnick May, K 2012, 'Some examples of how power posing can actually boost your confidence', TED Blog, blog.ted.com/10-examples-of-how-power-posing-can-work-to-boost-your-confidence.

Index

Accenture 12
accountability 40, 47-48
advisors 215
Alice in Wonderland 30
Allen, David 173
American Psychological Association 27, 97
Anne of Green Gables 92
appearance 104
applications 131-132, 155-159, 177-193
Aronson, Elliot 113
artificial intelligence (AI) 186-187
Ashe, Arthur 195
Astaire, Fred 138
Atami 4
attitude 132, 166-167
Australian Broadcasting Corporation (ABC) 163
Australian Graduate School of Management 217
authenticity 196-198

Bachelor of Arts 3
Bandura, Albert 96
Banks, Andrew 217
Bennett, Floyd L. 41
Bersin, Josh 171
Bloomberg LP 163
Bloomberg, Michael 163
body language 72-74
bouncing back 60-62
boundaries 77-78
Buddha 109
Buttrose, Ita 163
buzzwords 183

Camus, Albert 21
career objective 183
career stages 121-122
CareerBuilder 183
Chamorro-Premuzic, Tomas 171
Child, Julia 163
Clarke, Arthur C. 119
Clarke, Jane E. 53
cognitive abilities 171
communication 67-68
confidence 100-102, 165-166
cover letters 190-193
Covey, Stephen R. 41, 43, 45
COVID-19 10, 12, 37, 54-56, 153, 163-164, 168, 205
Cuddy, Amy 203

culture 136-137
curiosity 30-34
CVs 178, 180-182

Daimaru 15-16
David Jones 15-16
De Niro, Robert 167
degrees 17-18
Delamontagne, Dr Robert P. 162
dependability 39-51
development 13, 26-27, 183
Disney, Walt 25
dreaming 128-129
Drucker, Peter 37

education 17-18
emotional intelligence (EQ) 81, 83
Emotional Intelligence: Why It Can Matter More Than IQ 83
entitlement 137-138
EST10 8, 70, 136, 151, 153, 158, 205, 217
Eurich, Tasha 82
exercise 105
eye contact 73

Facebook 145
facial expressions 75-76
failure 62-63
feedback 83-85, 86-88, 132-133, 148
first job 134-140
Fisher, Donald 144
flexibility 157-158
Foundation for Young Australians 110, 126
Fraser, Dr Adam 62
freedom 50, 211-212
Freud, Sigmund 106

generations 165
Gladwell, Malcolm 29
global financial crisis (GFC) 55, 149, 168
goals 57, 105, 215
Goggins, David 92
Goleman, Daniel 65, 83
good for business 45-47
graduates 123-140
Grant, Adam 61
gratitude 104
growth 26-27

Haefner, Rosemary 183
Hall, Douglas T. 143
handshakes 73
Harvard Business Review 137
Harvard Medical School 111
Hendriksen, Dr Ellen 61
Herbert, Brian 28
human resources 3
humblebrag 199-200

immigration 164
Ingham, Harry 90
Insight: The Power of Self-Awareness in a Self-Deluded World 82
interning 131-133
interpersonal nous 65-79

interviews 195-209
—mistakes 207-208
Irving, Justine 163

Jagger, Mick 161
Japan 4-6, 68, 74, 217
job hunting 135-136
job readiness 124-127
Jobs, Steve 8, 123, 211
Johari window 90-92
Johnson, Whitney 145
Jordan, Michael 102
Journal of Career Assessment 146
Julia Ross Recruitment 7
Jung, Carl 99

knowledge 25-38

lateness 202, 204-205
learning 25-38, 215
—planning 35-36
—willingness 28-30
life expectancy 162, 164
LinkedIn 128, 129, 135, 156, 157, 184
listening 69-70
London 68, 115
longevity 126
long-term jobs 16-17
Luft, Joseph 90

Mad Max: Fury Road 163
malaise 145-147
Mandela, Nelson 53
manners 137-138
Manson, Mark 98
Masahide, Mizuta 109
Mensa 41
micromanagement 49
midcareer 141-150
Miller, George 163
Millman, Dan 19
Monash University 3, 217
Morgan, Geoff 217
Morrison, Scott 164
Mulhearn, Dijanna 202

negativity 114-116
nerves 195-196
networking 167
Nicholson, Dr John 53

nonverbal cues 72-77
observation 6
optimism 56-57, 109-117
organisation 139-140
Ostafin, Brian D. 56
outfits 202, 207
Outliers: The Story of Success 29
overconfidence 102-103
overseas, living 57-58

parental leave 153
parents 151-159
patience 124, 205
patterns 85
peace of mind 43-45
personal brand 127-128
pessimism 111, 116
Pollyanna 111
Pollyanna Principle 111
power pose 203-204

pragmatism 112
Pratfall Effect 113-114
preparation 105
pressure 40-41
Proulx, Travis 56
punctuality 202, 204-205
Pure Profile 125

qualifications 17-18
questions 200-201

recession 4
recruitment consultants 155-156
redundancy 14-16, 147-149
references 127-128, 184-185
reputation 127-128
research 198-199
resilience 53-64
—emotional versus practical 60
—how to build 55-58
Resilience: Bounce Back from Whatever Life Throws at You 53
responsibility 50
résumés 156-157, 178-179, 182-185, 187-190, 207-208
retiring 161-172
returning to work 151-159
Roosevelt, Theodore 95
Roshan, Hrithik 205
Ross, Julia 6-7, 217

salary 201
Savage, Greg 217
school leavers 123-140
SEEK 135
self-awareness 81-94
self-confidence 95-107
self-efficacy 96-97
self-esteem 96-97, 165-166
self-reflection 88-90
self-talk 103-104
Seligman, Martin 103, 112
Shakespeare, William 141
Sills, Beverly 177
Skype 205
smiling 73
St Maarten, Anthon 204
STAR method 182, 199
stress 47-48, 61

technical skills 34
technology 145, 156
Tehan, Hon. Dan 125
termination 147-149
The 7 Habits of Highly Effective People 41
The Gap 144
The Intern 167
The Power of Self-Confidence 96
The Retiring Mind 162
Theroux, Paul 39
tone 74-75
Tracy, Brian 96, 98, 105
trends 85
trust 41-43, 48-49
Tugaleva, Vironika 81
TwoPointZero 125

uncertainty 10-12
Universities Australia 125

University of Sydney 156, 217

video interviews 205-207

Wademan Dowling, Daisy 152-153
Wang, Vera 144
Wardrobe 101 202
Webjet 37
work experience 126, 131-133
Workparent 153
World Economic Forum 10

Zoom 10, 158, 205